Praise for *Sermon on th*

"Nicole Horsch's "Sermon on the Mount of Messy" is a practical devotional that takes the profound principles of the Scriptures and applies them to our everyday life. Nicole's insights are real, relatable, and transparent as she has the ability, through her own life experiences, to move you to self-introspect your own messes for the glory of God."

-Andrea Maher, author of *SLAMMED: Overcoming Tragedy in the Wave of Grief*

"We're a busy but needy people these days, which is why I greatly enjoyed the work of Nicole Horsch. In short digestible pieces, she was able to feed my soul with some much-needed nourishment in the Sermon of the Mount of Messy. If you need quality, Christ-centered encouragement, you will greatly enjoy Nicole's candid but poignant snippets of life. As an author myself, I'm convinced that Nicole and I would find much to muse over at a coffee shop—given it had late hours. Thank you Nicole!"

-Linda Lacour Hobar, author of *The Mystery of History*

"Sermon on the Mount of Messy is a must read! It is a powerful book with simple truths from the Word of God that are sure to comfort and challenge you all at the same time. It will draw you closer to the heart of Jesus as Nicole invites readers to see Him in all of his humanity and his divinity. Her fresh perspective of the Sermon on the Mount makes the Word come alive in a real and tangible way that will change your life."

-April N. Betner, CEO and Founder of April Betner Ministries, Inc.

"Get ready! If you are looking for a book that will meet you at your current mess and will Biblically guide you how to live victoriously as a child of God, read this! This author is raw and real. She will share some of her not so perfect moments and how God uses messes for His glory. This is an interactive book, so get your Bible, paper and pen because you are about to embark on a beautiful journey with the Lord."

-Isabel Mayer, Founder, Real Armored Women (RAW) Ministries

"Nicole is an inspiration to real women everywhere! She has just the right amount of humor and a realistic view of the world that makes this book an excellent read. Combine that with her spiritual depth and obvious love for the Lord and this book comes alive as an encouraging tool for spiritual insight and growth!"

-Tracy Endo, Certified Life Coach and Owner, NoVa Sports Coach, Competitive swim coach

"Beautiful, authentic, messy, raw... I seriously love this book! I breathe a sigh of relief as I read Nicole's writing - to know my "out-of-character" hidden self is allowed, acceptable and even encouraged – for it's in this place of realness, of putting all my cards on the table, that the darkness is brought out into the light and real transformation can begin. To read "Sermon on the Mount of Messy" is to feel like you are sitting across the table from a friend. She connects the scripture to real life and makes it so completely accessible! And in turn, I fall more in love with Jesus!"

- Suni Piper, Writer, Blogger, ASurrenderedLife.com, Contributing Writer, Intercessors for America

SERMON
ON THE MOUNT
OF
MESSY

E
M
J
PRESS

SERMON
ON THE MOUNT
—— OF ——
MESSY

NICOLE HORSCH

Foreword by Joanna Sanders, author of *Fire Women*

Cover Design: Propel Marketing LLC
Editing: Joanna Sanders LLC
Layout & Formatting: Propel Marketing LLC
Author's Photo Credit: Angela Wade, Wade Creatives
Press Logo Design: Andrea Horsch

ISBN 978-1-7351584-0-2 (Paperback)
ISBN 978-1-7351584-1-9 (eBook)

Dedication

To my husband for witnessing many miracles with me;

to my kids for growing me in Christ daily;

to my mom for early morning "talk shows" that yield more wisdom than Solomon could have hoped for;

to my dad for being an amazing earthly father;

to my brother for cheering me on;

to my friends who loved and pushed me forward;

to Kim for following me down rabbit holes;

to Joanna for riding the roller coaster with me;

for Jesus—because He gives eternal and abundant life.

Messes

Foreword

I MET NICOLE WHEN NEITHER OF US WANTED ANY MORE FRIENDS. It really doesn't get more honest than that. Clearly, the enemy was interested in trying to delay some of the good work, and some of the good laughs we've realized since then.

Sermon on the Mount of Messy has been one of those projects that has changed me more than I want to admit. While I'm honored to have been Nicole's editor, it really was more like I became a disciple who sat as she told me all that Jesus had done in her life, and in turn, opened my eyes to the ways He was working in my own life. I couldn't even edit this content without admitting that there were some changes needed in my own mess.

Nicole is honestly one of the funniest people I know. You will get a glimpse of that in her writing, but what's more important, is her authenticity. She is even going to be transparent about the times that she hasn't been transparent. She's relatable. She's as real on paper as she is in person, dolphin tattoo and all. She is a beautiful soul. But don't let that fool you. Her mess has been real. Her struggle has been so real. And her victory, because of Christ, undeniable.

In the Bible, The Sermon on the Mount begins by saying that Jesus went up on the mountain, and when He sat down, His disciples came to Him (Matthew 5:1).

Here in Nicole's writing, you will see a disciple that indeed watched and took in that whole process. She has translated it beautifully, in her life and in her writing, working out her salvation (Phil 2:12). She watched as He went up the mountain of calvary. She watched as He laid His life down, and she has brought to Him a heart that truly embodies all of the aspects that Jesus teaches about in the Beatitudes. She is a willing disciple who is brave enough to take an honest climb through her own mess to share with you, what the view looks like from the top of the mountain.

You will not leave without knowing that He is always worthy of our climb.

Joanna Sanders
Author, editor, friend, proud fellow owner of a messy life, redeemed.

Introduction

THE GREATEST SERMON JESUS EVER PREACHED WAS THE SERMON ON THE MOUNT. The greatest witness to His power and redemptive grace is His work in our messy lives.

This book serves as a witness to His power in my own messy life. Don't get me wrong, my life is bountiful, my husband is a handsome hunk of love, and my girls are exquisite. But in a world of perfect looking people, place settings and matching napkins, it's good to see and hear about the real messes that go on behind everyone's closed doors. This collection intends to serve as a realistic glimpse of life. And for Christians, it may be even harder for us to want to admit, own, and address our own mess.

The Bible says our messes aren't completely clean until we get to heaven. Which means we can never do enough to get into Heaven on our own. Once we accept Christ as our Savior, we take an active role in the work He has begun and is completing in us. Until the day when the work is done (Phil 1:6), we walk with Him and work out the salvation He has for us. Simply stated, we are a work in progress. And that progress, or sanctification process (fancy term for a holy clean up) is what allows us to grow in our walk with Him and truly enjoy and rejoice in the strength of the Lord. He is the One who ultimately gets all the credit for turning our mess into beautiful works of Christ.

The joy for us is the participation in that process. If you've never thought about it in this way, consider that you and the Creator of the entire world are participating together in creating a new thing— a new perspective, a new blessing, a new good work, a new and more exquisite version of you, out of the mess that is currently in front of you. As you participate, you are co-laboring alongside of Him in your very own world. What an amazing Savior that would allow us anywhere near His holy handiwork.

The goal of this book is for you to see the love of God and grace of His son Jesus Christ in the everyday. If you already know Him, I pray you know Him a little better through my honest mess. If you don't know Him, I pray He becomes your Savior, like He is mine. My hope is that either way you find it hard not to be changed when you realize there's a Savior in the middle of your mess.

You will have the opportunity to address your mess at the end of each reading. Don't expect to always be comfortable with what I encourage you to do. I've learned that comfortable is usually the place where I grow the least, and so I want to encourage us both to take a brave step outside of that. Listen with an open heart, and a teachable spirit and I know that the God I serve will be gracious to lead you into all truth (John 16:13).

I am praying for you as you take a walk with me now to see what He did in my mess, and to hopefully encourage you to be brave enough to look honestly at what He's doing in yours.

Nicole

Section 1

Blessed are the poor in spirit for theirs is the kingdom of heaven.

Matthew 5:3

Knowing Glances

I HAVE ONE CHILD WHO, AS A TODDLER, HAD AN UNEXPLAINED AVERSION TO TARGET. (We'll call her Lucy.) Each time I approached the front doors of Target, Lucy would stiffen as straight as a board and would refuse to sit in the seat on the top of the red cart. Encouraging, pleading, and even attempting to tickle her tummy to trick her into bending proved to be unsuccessful. Eventually, I would find some way to fold her up just enough to buckle her into the seat, and head off through the store. Lucy's storm of emotions would build and build at every turn of the cart. The most memorable of these trips included the fitting for new shoes.

The only thing that made these stormy outings more bearable were the knowing glances from those moms or grandmas who would spot me in the aisle, and shoot me a quick look of, "I got you, girl. You can do this."

There's a comradery out there among parents—because no matter our economic status, race, or religion, there are common experiences in the difficulty of raising children. Life doesn't let anyone off the hook. You can have all the money or resources in the world, but if your kid doesn't want to try on the Velcro princess shoe, she will ball her foot up so tight, you can forget getting it on.

Our pain is what connects us in our experiences, even at different stages. You might not be a toddler mom. Maybe you dropped your first kid off at college and made the tearful walk from the dorm to the parking lot, to an empty car. Or you're the husband who sits in the waiting room while your wife goes back for her second or third mammogram because they're not sure they're getting a clear picture of the mass that was found. If you look around, there's someone who's been there and done that. And if your eyes don't see another person to relate to, in the dorm elevator or in the waiting room, you can be assured there's One waiting to hear your prayer who can relate.

It might seem silly to think Jesus identifies with us. No, He was not a father to screaming toddlers but His disciples weren't much better at times. Hot-headed Peter could put his foot in his mouth faster than a toddler can throw a princess shoe. Jesus didn't leave a kid at college but He left His dear cousin who baptized Him, in prison; knowing John's head would soon be served on a platter. Jesus had no wife, but He wept over the death of a good friend.

In fact, there's no depth of our own pain that He hasn't experienced. How about betrayal? Which of us hasn't seen that nervous smile and quick kiss from a supposed friend that turns out to be the kiss of death? We've all had a friend or family member practice deceit. Betrayal burns in our hearts the most and seems to be the most difficult to forgive. Jesus catches our eye lovingly, and nods because He's been there, too. Judas sold him into the hands of those who'd nail him to the cross, for a mere 30 pieces of silver.

Hebrews 4:15 reminds us:

> *For we do not have a high priest who is*
> *unable to sympathize with our weaknesses, but one who in*
> *every respect has been tempted as we are, yet without sin.*

I used to focus on the fact that Jesus encountered all the bad stuff without sinning, so I should try harder to be perfect like Him. However, I recently realized the value of looking more to see the knowing glances of our High Priest as the beginning part of the Scripture references—the great reminder that I am never alone. I may mess it up. I may lose my temper, say a bad word (or two), and struggle with forgiving. This verse isn't calling us to try harder, it's the job of the Holy Spirit to enable us to act in the holiness we simply cannot muster on our own. And we have a God who, like us, experienced every heartache, temptation, and frustration we encounter. Our kind Savior is looking to catch our eye and remind us, He gets it.

Address the Mess:

Take a deep breath and nod at Him in prayer. Your prayer doesn't have to be verbose and high-minded. Sometimes the best prayer of all is, "Help me." Simple, concise, and honest. Imagine what He would say back at you if you could audibly hear His words.

Sermon Notes

_____

_____

_____

_____

_____

_____

_____

_____

_____

_____

_____

_____

_____

_____

_____

_____

_____

_____

_____

_____

_____

_____

_____

_____

_____

Be Prepared

I'M MARRIED TO AN EAGLE SCOUT. My husband has been away from the scouting world for several years but much of what he learned, sticks with him still today. Every impending storm results in a refreshing of batteries in flashlights. An upcoming vacation means multiple lists, generally consisting of a master list for the entire family and smaller lists for each family member. We do not pull out of the driveway until all the boxes are checked.

I'm more of a "fly by the seat of my pants" kind of girl. I think it might drive my husband a little crazy. I'm often snickering at the lists and saying things like, "We're just going to the beach, I know there's a Walmart somewhere." The reality is that I often find myself needing something last minute or stressing out and there he stands; with the item I need in his hand. He's really kind about it too, and doesn't say "I told you so," but I'm sure it's satisfying to him and his sense of preparation. Deep down, I'm really thankful for his lists.

One thing I was totally unprepared for was the extensive preparation involved in planning for a missions trip. As I sat in my first short-term missions meeting, I heard a lot of talk about the many aspects that the teams needed to consider, such as shots and immunizations, passports, fundraising, and prayer. We were given short summaries about each trip and an overview of the mission projects assigned for each team. As I sat there, I realized my husband's keen sense of preparation might just come in handy for me after all.

I was also amazed to realize how God was preparing me decades ago for this trip, and I didn't even know it. It was quite surprising to see that the little bit of French I learned in high school could help me understand the Creole language of the Haitian people. I also had the blessing of having one thing checked off the list because of an arrangement that God had made earlier. As it turns out, I had obtained a passport years ago that I didn't technically need. Even though our trip was in Hawaii, our family's travel agent advised us to get passports because travel guidelines were changing so frequently, she thought they would be an important backup to have. We didn't use the passports on the trip, and I was a little miffed at the expense and headache we went through at the time to get them. Yet I was able to check that box for the trip and say that I had a current passport already in hand because of that ordeal. I was prepared in advance.

God doesn't always prepare us in advance, sometimes we are completely surprised and ill-prepared for circumstances. But I am amazed at the grace He gives us when something we thought was useless, overlooked or a huge mistake, becomes an asset or a valued skill later on, in a way we didn't expect. I'm excited to discover more ways that God is preparing me now for the upcoming adventures in my future. I am praying that He wastes nothing in my life and makes it all useful for His purposes and His kingdom.

Address the Mess:

What are some things you've done in your life but haven't put them to full use? Like my passport, do you have a degree, certification, or credential you haven't used? Pray and ask God how He might have prepared you in advance for something great for Him. Chances are, there are some things in your life that were completed well in advance of their use. Dig into this idea. Pray and journal about how to make use of God's preparation.

Sermon Notes

_____

_____

_____

_____

_____

_____

_____

_____

_____

_____

_____

_____

_____

_____

_____

_____

_____

_____

_____

_____

_____

_____

_____

Throwback Thursdays

SOCIAL MEDIA HAS BROUGHT ABOUT MANY NEW PHENOMENA, such as selfies, hashtags, likes, and friend requests. One of my favorites is "Throwback Thursday." People take to Twitter, Facebook, and Instagram to post great photos of themselves from previous years, sometimes as little kids or from old high school portraits. Those married couples in the 1980s with big hair are among my favorites. The hashtag #tbt is added, and everyone has a great time reminiscing about the old fashions, hairstyles, or home decor.

Some of my best Throwback Thursday pictures include my brother and me as kids. He was long, lanky, and tow headed, and I was the cute little sister with pig tails. My brother was the typical older brother who would tickle me until I wet my pants and I was the typical little sister who made a sport out of annoying my older brother. I love looking at those old photos because they remind me of who we once were.

I would say the seven-year age gap has now closed and we consider each other very good friends. We connect over Facebook and email with our love for puns and word play. We check in with each other from time to time and commiserate over kid-raising and the challenges of parenting today. He still looks out for me. A couple of years ago when one of our cars caught fire, he actually found a buyer who paid us cash for what looked like a charred heap of metal and plastic. Apparently that car still had great value and he knew it, and he helped make something out of nothing for us. I think that's a good analogy for a testimony many of us could relate to—things that we thought very little of, and God saw great value.

Throwback Thursdays are a great reminder of a principle found in the Bible. All throughout Scripture, we are reminded to recall who we once were, to see where we have come, and finally to give God praise for His hand in it all. He makes our "nothings" and our failures into things of great value. Our testimony holds significant importance for the Kingdom. In the last book of the Bible, John has a vision of Satan finally being defeated. Revelation 12:10-11 says:

> *And I heard a loud voice in heaven, saying, "Now the salvation and the power and the kingdom of our God and the authority of his Christ have come, for the accuser of our brothers has been thrown down, who accuses them day and night before our God. And they have conquered him by the blood of the Lamb and by the word of their testimony, for they loved not their lives even unto death."*

While Christ's blood is the ultimate weapon against evil, our testimony also participates in the triumph. What an awesome God that allows us to participate in this battle in such a mighty way!

The foundation of our testimony is grace—unmerited favor, the gift of God which, combined with faith, is the basis of our salvation (Eph 2:8-9). I believe this is why both believers and non-believers can relate to the lyrics in the popular hymn, "Amazing Grace" by John Newton. The hymn was written as a reflection and a revelation of how lost and blind Newton once was, as slave trader. He describes how God's grace and mercy removed him of his fears and brought him to a safer place within the will of God. Many people identify with this song, regardless of where they are in their walk with the Lord.

Throwback for a moment and think about where you have been. I grew up in a Christian household, but I knew nothing of this thing called "grace" or even worse, that I needed it. My understanding of Jesus was that He died on a cross for my sins but that I really didn't need to consider that word "sin." Honestly, I understood it to be an old-fashioned word, and really, just a downer. However, I was consumed with trying to understand why I wasn't living in the joy I thought Christians were supposed to have. At the bottom of a pit of hopelessness, I cried out to God to show me who He was, because I wasn't getting it. I am grateful to say that my testimony includes overcoming insecurity, despair, immoral behavior, and pure selfishness.

I challenge you to think of what the Lord has brought you out of and where you are headed. Maybe you have overcome abuse or a terrible addiction. Maybe your fears once gripped you so tightly, that you were incapable of functioning, but the Lord taught you confidence. Perhaps you were once discontent and searching for something to fill a void in your life and you have now learned to be content in all things. Perhaps you are in the middle of your testimony, right at this very moment.

Address the Mess:

I challenge you to think about today and what today will look like, ten or twenty years *from now*. Think of the lyrics in that famous hymn, "I once was…" and imagine what you could say about yourself during this time, if you were ten years in the future. Where would you like to see yourself? Where do you need victory? Imagine a snapshot of today and the hashtag #tbt and try to visualize how God is moving in the testimony in progress, right here and now.

Sermon Notes

Rewrites and Edits

Sometimes I will hear a phrase in a song, sermon, or on TV and it will echo in my mind for days. That can be a gift, especially if it is something that uplifts me, but sometimes, it can drive me up a wall. When a part of Scripture gets "stuck," I like to give it more consideration, as though the Lord were trying to get me to understand more about it. This happened one day with the reference to Jesus as the "author and perfecter of our faith." Being a writer, I connected immediately with the title of "author" and looked to the Scripture to consider the context:

> *Therefore, since we are surrounded by so great a cloud of witnesses, let us also lay aside every weight, and sin which clings so closely, and let us run with endurance the race that is set before us, looking to Jesus, the author and perfecter of our faith, who for the joy that was set before him endured the cross, despising the shame, and is seated at the right hand of the throne of God.*
>
> *Hebrews 12:1-3*

From my own experience, I understand that authoring something means rewrites and edits. It's crucial in the writing process to mold words like clay to bring thoughts into the best shape and form possible for the reader. Writers want to convey ideas and inspire their readers by crafting the best sentences possible. So, I got to thinking and questioning, "Does God rewrite and edit our lives if He is the author?"

Some folks shy away from God because this is exactly what they imagine: a writer who adds plots twists and surprise endings. Some assume that just as their life is getting really good, God decides to shake things up and throw in some drama and tragedy. I don't believe that's how it works. Scripture confirms that God has a purpose for our lives; that He knew us before we were in our mother's womb and that He has good works prepared for us. The bad stuff and drama comes from the fact that we are part of the fallen world in which sin is still present. Further, we learn from stories like Joseph's, that God will even make something good come from evil that we've encountered in life.

So, what about rewrites and edits? If God has written our story long before our birth, then the words on our pages don't necessarily change. The purpose of our lives is set. What often needs to be edited and rewritten is our response to God's work in our life. God's Word never changes but ours certainly should. Instead of lying in bed ignoring His voice, we must respond, "Yes, Lord!" when He calls. And when given the choice to follow the Lord's path or follow the world, He allows us to make the choice. Remember those "Choose Your Own Adventure" books? Sometimes it isn't a major directional choice that we need to make but the decision in the moment to praise Him and thank Him even though we'd like to grumble and complain. We don't need to know the outcome of the circumstances to do that. The game changers are our responses to God's present work in our lives. And when our hearts are right, and in line with the Lord, we really can't ever choose the wrong adventure.

 Jesus is the Author and Perfecter who has crafted a beautiful message in the story of our lives. Our part is to make sure our responses to Him are loving and in line with His will. We achieve that by laying aside the weights of the world and the sin that holds us down—even if it requires several drafts to get it right.

Address the Mess:

Write down what you've been hearing from the Lord lately in your prayer time. Take a week to purposefully pray over each item. What can you do to respond to Him? If you're not hearing from Him, get into His word, start with Psalms or the Book of John. Write down the thoughts you have as you read.

Sermon Notes

_____

_____

_____

_____

_____

_____

_____

_____

_____

_____

_____

_____

_____

_____

_____

_____

_____

_____

_____

_____

_____

_____

_____

_____

_____

The Original Walking Dead

And Jesus cried out again with a loud voice and yielded up His spirit.

Then, behold, the veil of the temple was torn in two from top to bottom; and the earth quaked, and the rocks were split, and the graves were opened; and many bodies of the saints who had fallen asleep were raised; and coming out of the graves after His resurrection, they went into the holy city and appeared to many.

So, when the centurion and those with him, who were guarding Jesus, saw the earthquake and the things that had happened, they feared greatly, saying, "Truly this was the Son of God!"

Matthew 27:50-54 (NKJV)

THERE'S BEEN AN OBSESSION WITH ZOMBIES THE PAST FEW YEARS IN OUR COUNTRY. One recently popular TV drama, *The Walking Dead*, depicted life in an apocalyptic world overrun with zombies. Transparently, I don't watch shows like this. I'm a big chicken when it comes to spooky things. I tend to have nightmares and my mind doesn't shake free of images very easily.

Yet, while I don't watch shows about the dead walking around, I see it in real life. Whether it be folks who are lost and need to be found, or religious people who seek to earn God's love, not realizing that they only need to accept Christ's final work on the cross.

In the Matthew 27 verse here, there's a lot to consider. An earthquake shook the land. Some geologists estimate the quake would have been a 5.5 in magnitude. The massive, four-inch-thick veil that separated man from the presence of God was split in two from top to bottom—meaning man now had direct access to God, because of Jesus. And there are "saints" referenced that came out of their graves and started walking around!

> **Jesus died on a Friday and waited until Sunday to rise again but these people were set free the moment Jesus died.**

We tend to skip over this part of our retelling of the Easter story, because I think it's somewhat unfathomable. Do you realize these saints got their resurrection before Jesus received His? Jesus died on a Friday and waited until Sunday to rise again but these people were set free the moment Jesus died. Amazing! Imagine being witness to the once dead walking free. It's as if God, the master storyteller, was foreshadowing what would happen to His son a few days later, so that people would believe.

I wonder who these saints were and how long they had been dead. I wonder what their names were, and to whom did they first appear? Did their families and friends see them? Did they resume a normal life? The questions are endless and add to the awe and mystery of our God who seeks to let us know that He is in the business of resurrection.

I thought these saints were the original walking dead, however I realize that we are all the walking dead before we know Jesus. Without Christ, it's as if we cover ourselves with that four-inch-thick veil. We are separated from God and spiritually dead. When Christ enters the picture, we have life. 1 John 5:12 (NKJV) says, "*He who has the Son has life; he who does not*

> ## *I thought these saints were the original walking dead, however I realize that we are all the walking dead before we know Jesus.*

have the Son of God does not have life. "It's just that simple, without Christ, *we* are the walking dead.

Whether it be folks who are lost and need to be found, or religious people who seek to earn God's love, we only need to recognize that God requires nothing but trust and belief in His Son. It was nothing more than the yielding of His Son's spirit who broke those people out of their tombs. There were no works to be done, their resurrection was not earned, it was immediate. The same miracle awaits each and every one of us today.

Address the Mess:

Who in your life needs to be set free from their tomb of death? Set a reminder in your phone or write down their name and pray for their salvation fervently.

Sermon Notes

_____

_____

_____

_____

_____

_____

_____

_____

_____

_____

_____

_____

_____

_____

_____

_____

_____

_____

_____

_____

_____

_____

_____

Who Are You Wearing?

THE AWARDS SEASON FOR TELEVISION, MOVIES, AND MUSIC ALWAYS SEEM TO PROVIDE MUCH TO TALK ABOUT. The red-carpet interviews prior to the actual awards ceremonies tend to be more popular than the award shows. The world tunes in to watch the beautiful people make their way down the red carpet and stop for photos and interviews. The most common question in a red-carpet interview is, "Who are you wearing?" And then the star or starlet tells us which famous designer created the tuxedo or gown.

Genesis 25 and 27 contain the account of Jacob and Esau. These twins, born to Isaac and Rebekah, were promised to be contentious from the beginning. They were described as two nations warring in Rebekah's womb. The boys grew up at odds with one another. It didn't help, of course, that their parents played favorites and fueled the fire between them.

Esau was the firstborn of the twins and grew to be the favorite of his father Isaac. He was a man's man—an outdoorsman and a hunter. Rebekah preferred Jacob, who literally clung to his brother's heal as he left the womb, seemingly embracing an unwanted role of "second" as the second born. Jacob was quieter and meeker; a homebody, but his mom's favorite. Jacob had a disadvantage when it came to winning the favor of his father.

As it became clear that Isaac was getting on in years and would need to pass on his blessing, Jacob grew to desire more from his father. His mother Rebekah also hated to see her favorite son be second best. They devised a plan to trick dear old dad into blessing Jacob with everything that was rightfully Esau's. Taking advantage of Isaac's blindness, Rebekah got him comfortable with his favorite stew and then Jacob put on Esau's best clothes along with some animal skins so he would smell and feel like his hairy brother. If asked, "Who are you wearing?" he could have replied, "Tunic by Esau."

Isaac recognized the clothing of his favorite son, but Jacob sat before him, impersonating and smelling just like his brother. And because of Rebekah and Jacob's deceitful manipulation, Isaac bestowed all of the blessings meant for Esau, upon Jacob. When Esau found out, he became enraged and the family became even more divided—ultimately resulting in nations at war with one another.

Isaac delighted in the scent of his favorite son's clothing. God delighted in the sight and obedience of Jesus. But what about the clothing of God's Son? Our God is not blind—there is no tricking or manipulating Him to present ourselves as something we're not. He sees our sin clearly, and He knows us better than we know ourselves. So, He tells us plainly what He'd like us to do in His Word. He says that because He sent His *one and only* son, that whoever believes in Him will have eternal life (John 3:16). Basically, the Father is saying to us, "Put on the clothes of my favorite Son and I will see your sin no longer. You will feel and smell just like my Son so that I will forget what you've done, and you will receive the blessings meant for Him. I will share the blessings with you, even though you don't deserve them. Just put on the clothes."

I could really care less about the Oscars and what these people wear. I find it silly that our culture becomes so fixated on the suits and gowns we could never afford or have occasion to wear. But I do care about what the Lord thinks of me. He's not just the Creator of the universe, but our Heavenly Father, our dad. He loves us all so much that He hands us the clean, pure white garment and says, "Go ahead, wear it...I have an occasion for you to attend. I want you with Me forever. Dine at My table. Feast with Me." What love, that He sees us as we are, and clothes us with His righteousness, so we can receive undeserved blessings.

As I step out each day, I decide what to wear and put on. I made a choice many years ago to accept Christ and put on His clothes. But it wasn't until the past fifteen years or so, that I really understood what it meant to wear Christ. Only by the sacrifice of His only Son, do I get to wear the lovely clothes to stand before my Father who accepts me as His own. I don't need to concern myself with the red carpet of the world, because I can walk down any path, in the confidence of God's favor upon me—the favor I never deserved by my own merit, bestowed on me, because of Who I wear.

> *Only by the sacrifice of His only Son, do I get to wear the lovely clothes to stand before my Father who accepts me as His own.*

Address the Mess:

Be honest—have you accepted Christ? Have you accepted the pure, white garment offered by His sacrifice on the cross? You're not a Christian just because your parents were or because you go to church. You are a Christ follower, a true Christian, when you confess with your mouth that Christ died on the cross for *your sins* and that you trust in Him and nothing else for your salvation (Romans 10:9). Have you said those words? If not, do it now. Then tell someone! You've got a new wardrobe! Walk with your head high knowing you belong to Jesus!

Maybe you accepted Christ but you forgot about the new clothes. Take time to reflect on the cross and the salvation you have. Replace whatever defeated feelings you are walking around with, (old clothing), instead with the truth of God's grace.

Sermon Notes

_____

_____

_____

_____

_____

_____

_____

_____

_____

_____

_____

_____

_____

_____

_____

_____

_____

_____

_____

_____

_____

_____

_____

_____

Adjustable

I WAS PUTTING SOME ICED TEA GLASSES AWAY THE OTHER DAY AND I BEGAN TO CURSE THE MAKERS OF MY KITCHEN CABINETS. The glasses wouldn't fit, and I began to say to myself, "How could someone make kitchen cabinets that do not accommodate iced tea glasses?!" Ridiculous.

And then that still, small voice kindly said, "Nicole, look inside that cabinet, Honey." (I'm thankful that the still, small voice is kind and calls me, Honey, and not, Idiot.) Inside my cabinet, there were little holes that ran from the bottom of the cabinet to the very top. I realized that the shelves sit on top of little clips that fit inside those holes. Eureka! I discovered that the shelves were adjustable. I paid a mortgage for 16 years but never knew about my adjustable shelves. Sometimes I'm not really sure I'm qualified to be a grown-up.

Like Dorothy, who had the power to get back to Kansas all along, I had the power to change my shelves. I suppose most of us go about our lives, yelling at our Maker like I yelled at my cabinet maker. We say things like, "Why am I like this?" or "How come this situation won't change?" With Christ in us and a little quiet-time

> **With Christ in us and a little quiet-time in our life, we have the opportunity to listen to the Maker and welcome Him to make adjustments in our lives. We are adjustable.**

43

in our life, we have the opportunity to listen to the Maker and welcome Him to make adjustments in our lives. We are adjustable.

The Bible reminds us that we are nothing but clay. We can be changed, and we can be remade over and over, if we submit to God's plans and His will for our lives.

> *Yet you, Lord, are our Father. We are the clay; you are the potter; we are all the work of your hand.*

> *Isaiah 64:8 (NIV)*

> *Remember that you molded me like clay. Will you now turn me to dust again?*

> *Job 10:9 (NIV)*

> *Woe to those who quarrel with their Maker, those who are nothing but potsherds among the potsherds on the ground. Does the clay say to the potter, 'What are you making?' Does your work say, 'The potter has no hands?'*

> *Isaiah 45:9 (NIV)*

and finally, Jeremiah 18:4 (NIV):

> *But the pot he was shaping from the clay was marred in his hands; so the potter formed it into another pot, shaping it as seemed best to him.*

It's not enough to simply acknowledge the Potter, we are to submit to Him. When we see that change needs to be made, we need to remember that He will remake us as it seems best *to Him*. That may mean you make some changes that you don't particularly like. You may need to give up habits or relationships you don't want to remove, but deep down you know that it would be better. Perhaps you begin praying and studying God's Word to learn what *His best* looks like, in comparison to what the world says is best.

Sometimes I picture myself like the pot on the wheel that seems almost finished, but the potter sees a flaw and allows that mass of clay to collapse on the fast-moving wheel. It looks like failure and a mess! But then the potter lovingly takes that clay in His hands again and begins to carefully turn the pot and shape and mold it into something more beautiful than before.

Don't be like me, standing in the kitchen yelling at the cabinet maker. Remember that God made us to change and to fall apart, only to be made more beautiful. Sometimes the changes don't hurt too badly and are actually quite simple. And then, just like that, your iced tea glasses fit quite nicely.

Address the Mess:

What do you blame God for?

Seriously. Just say it. Say it out loud. "I blame God for…"

Now, re-word that statement: "This (issue, area of life, painful memory, stronghold) can be different. And today, I'm going to do something about it."

Are you missing something that is so obvious and simple, like I was, with my shelves? Take a step back and look at the situation from a different perspective. What is one small thing you could do today to change the way you think and talk about this area of your life?

Now do it.

Sermon Notes

_____

_____

_____

_____

_____

_____

_____

_____

_____

_____

_____

_____

_____

_____

_____

_____

_____

_____

_____

_____

_____

_____

Section 2

Blessed are those who mourn for they shall be comforted.

Matthew 5:4

Couponing and Dumpster Diving

FROM THE BACK OF THE CAR, MY KID SNICKERED A BIT. She said, "Hey Mom, remember when you'd go to the recycling center and climb in those dumpsters to get newspapers for coupons? That was fun wasn't it?" As tears pricked my eyes and burned my nose, I muttered, "Yeah." I struggled because I realized my kid thought her mom was being eccentric—as though it was some hobby I was into, like scrap booking or Sudoku. She didn't know the reality of the situation.

The truth was, at the time we had very little money for groceries. I had to make our budget go as far as it possibly could, and utilizing coupons helped a great deal with that. As I got more efficient learning how to "coupon," I learned that many people threw out their Sunday papers and I could forage through the dumpsters at the recycling center to get extra copies of coupons.

I looked ahead and took a deep breath. I was ashamed to tell my kids the real story. I didn't want them to think less of their mom and dad for struggling financially. In that moment, I had a choice to make. Through tears, I looked in the rear-view mirror at her face and I said, "You know, Mom didn't really want to do that. But Mom was able to get enough coupons to be able to afford groceries because at that time in our life, we really couldn't afford groceries."

My kid looked out her window and just said, "Oh. Well that was pretty cool that you knew how to do that." My other daughter chimed in and said, "Remember how you used to teach us how to cut with scissors by cutting out the coupons?"

That was it. They were not embarrassed or ashamed of their mom. They pointed out my resourcefulness and how I always found a way to turn something into a home-schooling lesson. I was afraid of sharing this difficult reality in our family, but they had nothing but fond memories.

Today, I don't have to dumpster dive for coupons. Times can still be tight, but we are blessed beyond measure. We are able to give generously, pay our bills on time, and accomplish projects around our home. This doesn't mean there won't be difficult times again, but I remember where we once were, and how faithful God was to bring us through it. I also learned that my kids are more grace-filled than me when it comes to remembering. As a mom, I can beat myself up over hard times or times when I thought I did a bad job.

There is something very beneficial to our souls to reflect and remember where we once were. Part of living a life of gratitude and thanksgiving is to look back at some of the hard times. And sometimes we even get a different view of how God used them.

Address the Mess:

It's important to be honest with our children when sharing the past with them. It's an opportunity to show them how the Lord has worked in their life and to show His faithfulness. Psalm 138 (GNB) is a great expression of thanksgiving:

> *I thank you, Lord, with all my heart;*
> *I sing praise to you before the gods.*
> *I face your holy Temple, bow down, and praise your name*
> *because of your constant love and faithfulness, because*
> *you have shown that your name and your commands are*
> *supreme.*
> *You answered me when I called to you;*
> *with your strength you strengthened me.*
> *All the kings in the world will praise you, Lord,*

because they have heard your promises.
They will sing about what you have done and about your
great glory.
Even though you are so high above, you care for the lowly,
and the proud cannot hide from you.
When I am surrounded by troubles, you keep me safe.
You oppose my angry enemies and save me by your power.
You will do everything you have promised;
Lord, your love is eternal.
Complete the work that you have begun.

Use this Psalm to honestly recount the Lord's faithfulness in your life. Looking back, can you see any major events from a different perspective?

Sermon Notes

_____

_____

_____

_____

_____

_____

_____

_____

_____

_____

_____

_____

_____

_____

_____

_____

_____

_____

_____

_____

_____

_____

_____

_____

When Your Smile Changes

EVERY MOTHER'S DAY, FACEBOOK TRADITION CALLS FOR CHANGING YOUR PROFILE PICTURE TO HONOR YOUR MOM. One Mother's Day weekend, I clicked through lots of pictures trying to find one of my mom and me together. It's rare we are in photos together, because like most moms, one of us is usually taking the picture. I finally found a suitable photo from seven years ago and changed my profile picture. However, I stared into my face and I noticed something different. I don't smile like that anymore. My grin was much wider then, and my smile rose deep into my eyes. I looked at more current photos of me and noticed the smiles aren't like that anymore. Sometimes I'll grin if prompted, but generally I must be prodded a bit to "say cheese."

Many people speculate about the intriguing smile of the Mona Lisa. I personally think Mona Lisa was a wise woman who knew a lot about the world and her smile wasn't so much about being coy, or shy, but simply a statement that she knew a thing or two. That she was naive no longer.

Time brings about many changes. For me, our marriage had gone through so much. Life and death had happened. And in between, I had attempted to gather the wisdom that had been scattered about after the breaking and bruising of hearts. I have come to understand that the knowledge and understanding left from these experiences had changed me. If my new smile had a caption it could be, "I know a little too much about the world now." Naïve no longer.

Don't get me wrong. I wouldn't change a thing, nor do I regret what I've experienced. God has refined me with His fire—one meant to bring impurities to the surface and remove them in order to create a finer, stronger metal. I have grown now to appreciate images and memories in a new way. I've learned that there is a lot more to a photograph than a cheesy grin or a smug mug. There is a story behind our eyes.

> **If my new smile had a caption it could be, "I know a little too much about the world now." Naïve no longer.**

Job spent a lot of time thinking about his life and contemplating his situation. I was struck by his comment about his current losses and feeling as though God was judging him. He said:

> *"My days are swifter than a runner; they fly away without a glimpse of joy. They skim past like boats of papyrus, like eagles swooping down on their prey. If I say, 'I will forget my complaint, I will change my expression, and smile.'*

Job 9:25-27 (NIV)

Job knew a thing or two about life. He had endured a lot. I suspect had there been photography then, his smile would have been quite different before and after his trials. When you've been through some stuff, your expression and your smile changes.

Address the Mess:

Sometime soon take some honest pictures with your family. What's really happening? No need to stage an Instagram-perfect moment just be real. Document this time and if there's joy, give thanks, and if there's pain, bring it before the Lord.

Sermon Notes

Greenhouse Effect

Do not despise these small beginnings, for the Lord rejoices to see the work begin, to see the plumb line in Zerubbabel's hand.

Zechariah 4:10 (NLT)

I WAS BLESSED TO SPEND ONE MORNING AT A LOCAL FARM that grows food for families who cannot afford fresh produce and quality meats. I toured the farm and learned how they produce tens of thousands of pounds of food very efficiently while stewarding God's resources. At the end of the tour, the group I was with packed thousands of pounds of sweet potatoes that would be delivered to local area food banks. While this activity was wonderful, I was really captivated by what I learned in the greenhouse.

We stepped inside of what appeared to be a standard greenhouse, and the farmer explained how they start seeds for the upcoming crops. I learned that the seeds are started in the greenhouse, but they don't finish their growth there. The crops must make their way outside where the elements can help them grow best. They must move out to make room for new seeds to grow. This greenhouse also keeps the climate at a constant temperature, while shielding the vulnerable seeds from extreme temperatures, critters, and even from getting too much water. The sides of this greenhouse automatically raise and lower to allow cooler air in if the temperature gets too high. I marveled at the state-of-the-art technology used to get the lettuce, squash, and other crops started.

This experience reminded me that God almost never intends for us to stay in the same place for too long. He uses our education, our faith, our experiences, and even our tragedies to move us out of safe spaces into the bigger, wider world so that we can grow to our fullest potential and ultimately feed those who hunger for truth and grace. As Christians, it can be tempting to hide out in the state-of-the-art greenhouses that keep our lives typical and predictable, but if we look at the examples God gives us in His Word, the most impactful believers never stayed anywhere too long.

Abraham was told to go to a place that God would show him, and the result was that Abraham would have too many descendants to count. Joseph went from the safe fold of his father's flock to the dungeon, and then to the palace of an Egyptian pharaoh where he would ultimately feed his starving family of origin and nation. Esther went from the safe home of her cousin as an orphan, to the palace of the king where she would prevent the genocide of her people. Paul traveled almost constantly on ministry. And Jesus never stayed anywhere too long. He had no place to lay His heavenly head and He went about His travels being challenged by the opposition, but he continued to heal and save the dying world. Isaiah 61:3 (NIV) says:

> *...and provide for those who grieve in Zion—to bestow on them a crown of beauty, instead of ashes, the oil of joy, instead of mourning, and a garment of praise, instead of a spirit of despair.*

> *They will be called oaks of righteousness, a planting of the Lord for the display of his splendor.*

We might be grieving and mourning in this world, but God has bigger plans for us. We are all called to be mighty oaks, but an oak can't be contained within a small greenhouse. Eventually that seedling must be taken out and planted firmly beside Living Water so that it can stretch towards the sun. Oaks provide shelter for many vulnerable creatures and continue to produce their own fruit so future generations can be brought forth.

I imagine it's a shock for the little seedings to be taken out to be planted.

The farmer even explained they use a high-powered pressure planter to make sure the seedings are dropped securely into the soil so the roots can be established. I bet those first few days out of the greenhouse are uncomfortable for those tender plants. Yet those vegetables will never nourish anyone if they don't get out of the greenhouse and grow!

Address the Mess:

So, what's your greenhouse? Consider your safe place where you are most comfortable, sheltered and possibly, in control. Is it your job, your school, your church? Maybe you've been doing ministry the same way as long as you can remember, and something doesn't feel quite right. Examine your environment, is it automatic? God never intends for our faith to be automatic, it should be exciting, sometimes a little uncomfortable, or downright scary. Nevertheless, He promises to grow us into mighty oaks if we allow ourselves to step out in faith.

Sermon Notes

_____
_____
_____
_____
_____
_____
_____
_____
_____
_____
_____
_____
_____
_____
_____
_____
_____
_____
_____
_____
_____
_____
_____
_____
_____

Don't Look Back

THE BIBLE IS FULL OF STORIES OF PEOPLE AND GROUPS RUNNING FROM THINGS. Jacob ran from Esau. The Israelites fled the Egyptian army. David ran from hot-headed Saul. And Lot's family fled Sodom and Gomorrah as fire and sulfur rained down on this despicable place.

Abraham's son, Lot, settled his family in Sodom and Gomorrah for a while, but these towns were known for some of the most wicked human behavior. When the Lord sent two angels to warn and rescue the family before the city's destruction, the men in the town pounded on Lot's door because they wanted to rape the angels. (I'm not making this up! Read Genesis 19 for yourself. The Bible is not a boring book!) Lot kept the door shut as the crowds pushed and pounded, demanding that the two men (angels) be brought out for violent sexual escapades.

The angels blinded the men who sought to violate them. They then directed Lot to take his daughters and wife and escape the city before God brought mass destruction. The angels gave specific instruction, "Escape for your life. Do not look back or stop anywhere in the valley. Escape to the hills, lest you be swept away" (Gen 19:17). Lot even tried to negotiate how far he was required to run, making it quite obvious he didn't realize how important it was to distance himself from this place and these people.

Have you ever been prompted to leave a situation, but you only went a short distance away? Perhaps you ended a friendship in person, but you continued to interact online. Maybe you quit a habit that was harmful to yourself or your family, but remained close friends with those who partake in it. Maybe you were prompted to physically move away from toxicity, yet you only removed yourself emotionally. Sometimes God requires drastic changes to protect ourselves and our families.

In this Biblical account, God had finally had enough. As Lot and his family began to flee, fire and sulfur fell from heaven. The fiery hail and sulfur would destroy everyone and everything in its path. One scientist compares the destruction of this scene to that of a hydrogen bomb. It must have been a spectacle, something cataclysmic! I imagine that although the people there were horrendous, Lot's family, specifically Lot's wife, likely cared for someone behind them. Maybe there was a neighbor who shared bread, or sat at their table. Maybe there were some children they helped look after. Even though their experience there might have been hard and ugly most of the time, I wonder if Lot's family felt like it would have been easier to stay in a horrible situation because it was familiar? I know I have struggled in this way before and needed God to intervene to show me the importance of exiting from it. The angels knew this was the case for Lot and wanted to get him and his family out of Sodom, before Sodom became too much a part of them.

However, Lot's wife neglected the specific instruction from the angels, and, as they fled, she looked back. She immediately became a pillar of salt. A statue. Rendered useless. A monument to the ungodly attachment that needed to die.

God never wastes instruction and while we may have our own feelings about a situation, when He tells us to run, we can be assured it is for good reason. We are not to look back and cling to a mess, because ultimately, we become part of the mess ourselves. If we are not careful, we become a relic of the former times, instead of the new creation He intended us to be.

Many a motivational speaker will tell you that the windshield of your car is larger than the rear-view mirror for a reason. We cannot safely operate a vehicle if we cannot see clearly what is in front of us. The rear-view mirror serves as a way to check and remember where we've been and to help us see who or what is following us. However, if we drive with our eyes on that

rear-view mirror constantly, we
will wreck ourselves and others.
Remaining in the past renders us
powerless and ineffective to our
family in the present, and ultimately, to God's kingdom in the
future.

Sadly, it appears that even
though Lot and his daughters
escaped safely, they continued
in dysfunction. Instead of living

> *Remaining in the past renders us powerless and ineffective to our family in the present, and ultimately, to God's kingdom in the future.*

out the freedom God offered, Lot fearfully hid himself in a cave with his
daughters where they recreated their own version of Sodom. Deception and
incest would now be permanently written into their story.

Sodom had become such a part of them, that it did not end even with the
geographic separation. Even though they physically had not looked back,
their hearts hadn't left. God does not only demand physical and practical
changes in our lives, but also genuine heart change. He requires our full
commitment to the instructions He's provided – not just the outward appearance of such.

The children born out of this dysfunction were the fathers of idolatrous
nations who committed human sacrifices. The threads of Sodom were wo-
ven deep within this family. Thankfully, God knew that man needed help
because left to our own striving and attempts to clean up our act, we fail
miserably, such as this family did. We tend to either look back or we repeat
the failures even after we believe we have separated from them. Jesus Christ
comes to stand between the past and the future. He comes to walk with us
out of the prison and into promise.

Address the Mess:

Whether you're being told to run, are in the middle of the escape or you are
remembering the former life; meditate on this promise and what it means
for you:

Therefore, if anyone is in Christ, he is a new creation. The old has passed away; behold, the new has come.

2 Corinthians 5:17

Now, consider what needs a drastic change in your life. (And no, the answer is not to eat more greens or exercise more! Those are good things, but for this mess, we need to focus on what needs to be cut away.) What person, place, or thing needs a permanent boundary put into place? Have the hard conversation, quit the toxic work environment, or put the bottle down and find the 12-Step meeting. Whatever it takes, your future starts now! Don't look back.

Sermon Notes

_____

_____

_____

_____

_____

_____

_____

_____

_____

_____

_____

_____

_____

_____

_____

_____

_____

_____

_____

_____

_____

_____

_____

Seasons Change

There is a time for everything,
and a season for every activity under the heavens:
a time to be born and a time to die,
a time to plant and a time to uproot,
a time to kill and a time to heal,
a time to tear down and a time to build,
a time to weep and a time to laugh,
a time to mourn and a time to dance,
a time to scatter stones and a time to gather them,
a time to embrace and a time to refrain from embracing,
a time to search and a time to give up,
a time to keep and a time to throw away,
a time to tear and a time to mend,
a time to be silent and a time to speak,
a time to love and a time to hate,
a time for war and a time for peace.

Ecclesiastes 3:1-8 (NIV)

L IFE IS MADE UP OF SO MANY DIFFERENT TYPES OF SEASONS. There are seasons related to time of year, time of growth and adulthood, times of parenting, and even times of relationships. We find ourselves in seasons and we often find ourselves just as quickly, longing for a change. As soon as we flip, we are ready to flop. Some seasons feel longer than others. Some seasons feel way too short. Here in Virginia, we only get a few days of *real* spring weather. We seem to dive headfirst into hot, humid summer days directly from the cold of winter. So, when the warm, gentle spring breezes occasionally grace us, we run outside to play and turn our faces to the sky wishing it would last forever. A couple of days later, we hide from the sun and praise Jesus for air conditioning. If I were writing Ecclesiastes from my perspective, my version would sound more like this:

> *There is not enough time in the day and too much to do in*
> *that time.*
> *There's a time to clean and time to be sloppy,*
> *a time to be thin and a time to be plump.*
> *a time to be taut and time to be flabby,*
> *a time for obedient children and a time for sass,*
> *a time for savings and a time for debt.*
> *a time to adore and a time for indifference.*
> *a time for enthusiasm and a time for meh.*

God speaks of seasons all throughout the Bible. He points out rainy seasons and dry seasons; seasons of work and harvest, and periods of rest. Timing is everything to God. Time has a purpose, and is not to be dreaded. Even when we are within God's will there will be arid times, times of need, and times of turmoil. It's the ebb and flow of life. So why do we fight it so much?

I think deep down, every human being longs for something that will last forever. We want financial security forever, health forever, good relationships, forever. If you continue reading in Ecclesiastes 3, you will read that God has "set eternity in man's heart." We were designed to long for the eternal. But so often, we place eternal emphasis in the wrong places.

When we finally realize that the grass withers and the flowers fall, we learn to seek the eternal in Jesus Christ—the only promised eternal security. Whether birth or death, beginning or end, old or young, winter or summer, He is there. He is every season.

Even though I am a believer in Jesus and His Word, I find myself struggling with earthly seasons and the peace of heavenly eternity. I can be distracted and discouraged by my present troubles and not remember the safety, security and peace of heaven that awaits. Sometimes life here feels like eternal winter. But there, every season will have us basking in the Son that never sets.

Address the Mess:

> *When we finally realize that the grass withers and the flowers fall, we learn to seek the eternal in Jesus Christ— the only promised eternal security.*

What season or seasons in your life have you most dreaded? They may be seasons that have already passed. If so, name the three most valuable aspects of them, looking at them in hindsight. If they are seasons that are yet to come, name the three biggest fears or apprehensions that you have about them and then go find a Bible verse that specifically relates to each concern. Seasons are inevitable. Prepare your house well now, for the seasons that are to come.

Sermon Notes

_____

_____

_____

_____

_____

_____

_____

_____

_____

_____

_____

_____

_____

_____

_____

_____

_____

_____

_____

_____

_____

_____

_____

_____

_____

Section 3

Blessed are the meek for they shall inherit the earth.

Matthew 5:5

Awkward Introductions

MY KIDS LOVE IT WHEN I TELL THEM FUNNY STORIES about times when I have embarrassed myself. I was able to entertain them with the tale of how I met my best friend, Callie, in college. Meeting Callie was one of the most awkward moments of my life. Recently, my children found great humor in realizing that their very social mother could be a social disaster.

It was the first weekend of our freshman year at Frostburg State University. While most students were sleeping off whatever they had done the night before, I woke up fairly early Saturday morning hungry for breakfast but not knowing how to get breakfast. I ventured down to the lounge in our dorm and sat wondering how I would get to the dining hall. Would I have to go alone? I hated eating alone. And there came Callie. And she sat in the same area of the lounge. And we sat. In silence.

I don't remember who had the brilliant idea first, but someone said, "Want to go to breakfast?" And the other said, "Ok." Thus, commenced the longest half-mile walk across the campus and down the hill to the Chesapeake Dining Hall, in silence. There were no, "Where'd you go to high school?" or "What are you majoring in?" type of discussions. Nothing, just silence. We entered the dining hall, which smelled like maple syrup, joined by the sound of the clanging trays and silverware.

Continuing in silence, we chose our meal and then a table, where I sat down and began to inspect the silverware. Yep, I did that. I looked at each piece of silverware with disgust as I scraped remnants of the last person's meal from my fork. I got up and got new silverware and then inspected again. Callie watched me and said nothing. Then I began to eat and sniffed each bite of food before I put it in my mouth, sort of like Hawkeye Pierce from the TV show, MASH. I sniffed it! In silence. We chewed and swallowed and sipped, in silence.

Eventually, our long, silent meal was over, and we made our way back up the hill to our dorm and disappeared into our rooms separately. I thought, *there is no way this girl could ever like me, what was wrong with me?* Well, oddly enough, we became the best of friends. At some point, the silence was broken, and we discovered each other's sense of humor. Ironically, our styles became so similar that we were often mistaken for each other on campus! Other students would be confused when they saw us together because they thought we were the same person. Throughout the years of our friendship, we have been in each other's weddings and Callie has held every one of my babies within hours of their birth. We've come a long way from that silent trek to the dining hall.

So, what's this got to do with Jesus? I think many of us have had awkward introductions to Jesus. Some of us were dragged to church by our parents and made to sit upright while listening to a bunch of boring stuff and weird music. Some of us were introduced to a harsh Jesus who seemed more like a judge producing followers who were more angry than happy to be "saved" by Him. Some of us never got introduced at all despite being placed right in front of others who were in positions to provide the perfect introduction to Him –like standing between a new person and an old friend, waiting for an introduction that never comes. Awkward. Not how God intended us to meet his Son.

We were meant to discover that He is kind and merciful and loving. We were meant to look past the strange and sinful ways of the people around Him to just see Him and hear His words of grace of forgiveness. Somehow, Callie was able to look past my silverware-scraping, pancake-sniffing-self and see who I was underneath. With one or two more tries, we were able to meet the real friend God had waiting for us.

Many people think the book of Revelation is the scariest book in the Bible.

74

They consider that it is filled with images of destruction and wrath. Yet one of the best pictures of our Savior is tucked in Revelation. Revelation 3:20 says, "Behold, I stand at the door and knock. If anyone hears my voice and opens the door, I will come into him and eat with him, and he with me."

Christ didn't come to be harsh and hurtful. And He definitely didn't come to be awkward. He came to have a relationship with us. Jesus just wants to dine, even if you sit in silence and don't know what to say. Or you're weird and you sniff your food. He doesn't care, He just wants to be asked to the table.

Addressing the Mess:

Think of someone in your life you have a weird relationship with. It could be a family member but it could also be the cashier at the grocery store – the more awkward, the better! (I know you just squirmed in your seat. I understand.) Invite that person to coffee or lunch, and dine with them. Ask them how they are doing and get to know them. You don't have to sign up for a two-week vacation with them, just 30 minutes of coffee and a muffin.

Next, do the same thing with Jesus. Whether in the privacy of your own home or at the coffee shop, dine with Him. You can set His place or place your Bible where His plate might go. As weird as it sounds, talk to Him. Not wordy, flowery "thou" and "hath" prayers but a real conversation with the same things you'd say to a friend. "This is bugging me" or "What do I do about so and so?" And then sit and listen with your heart.

What table are you sitting at today that you can invite Him to? Consider making a habit out of dining with someone else and with Jesus regularly. We were made to be in relationship with others and most importantly, with Him.

Sermon Notes

_____

_____

_____

_____

_____

_____

_____

_____

_____

_____

_____

_____

_____

_____

_____

_____

_____

_____

_____

_____

_____

_____

_____

_____

Learning Through Lameness

Jesus went on from there and walked beside the Sea of Galilee. And he went up on the mountain and sat down there. And great crowds came to him, bringing with them the lame, the blind, the crippled, the mute, and many others, and they put them at his feet, and he healed them, so that the crowd wondered, when they saw the mute speaking, the crippled healthy, the lame walking, and the blind seeing. And they glorified the God of Israel.

Matthew 15:29-31

W E HAD THE PRIVILEGE AND MASSIVE RESPONSIBILITY of owning a horse for a while. Our daughters were heavily involved in horseback riding and they enjoyed time in the barn caring for the horses. They took great pride in caring for their very own horse. Unfortunately, our spunky mare was often unable to work because she came up lame.

Lameness in horses is defined as "an abnormal stance or gait caused by either a structural or a functional disorder of the horse's loco-motor system."[1] A horse suffering from lameness will be unwilling or unable to stand or move normally. Sometimes it's general soreness and other times it's the result of a much bigger problem, such as an injury or illness. Because horses

---

1   Adams, Stephen. "Overview of Lameness in Horses", www.merckvetmanual.com. October 2015. Accessed May 24, 2020

can't tell us what's going on, veterinarians put the horse through tests to determine treatment. Our horse often went through exams where she would be made to walk, trot, or canter, and we would carefully watch her gait to see which leg or shoulder was the culprit.

> *It's a whole lot easier to notice a person who is limping along spiritually or emotionally, when you've been there yourself.*

When you have had a horse who was lame as often as ours was, it becomes easier to spot other horses with injuries and lameness as well. Sadly, through our experience, we became experts at pointing out horses that were struggling. I've noticed this also applies to people. It's a whole lot easier to notice a person who is limping along spiritually or emotionally, when you've been there yourself.

I was once at an event where my friend confided in me that she was pretty sure an individual in attendance was drunk. I asked her how she knew, and she said, "because my nose knows." My friend grew up with an alcoholic father, so she had become quite sensitive to the behavior and smell of someone who's been hitting the bottle pretty hard. This friend can spot alcoholism easily when others might not notice.

Maybe you don't quickly recognize an alcoholic, but you might know what a physically or emotionally battered wife looks like. You might notice a child with a learning disability because of the hours you struggled with your own child. Perhaps you can tell by a woman's shopping cart that money is tight because your own basket looked similar a few years back. If we're honest about our own brokenness and hurts, it's really not hard to see there are people who are struggling in the same way.

 Miracles occur when people use their own lameness or brokenness to see others, acknowledge them, stand by them without judgement, and sit with them in their messes. Our society is so polished and seemingly-perfect and filtered, that people are walking around lame and crippled and no one is seeing them. I imagine they feel a lot like my feisty mare who was often hurt but couldn't tell me with words.

What if we made more time to learn from, and acknowledge our own lameness, *and then* minister to those around us who might have the same struggles? On lookers might be amazed, and look with wonder, and perhaps even glorify the God of Israel.

Address the Mess:

Where are you lame right now? Is it finances, relationships, or maybe your health? Be honest. Where are you limping along? Bring it to the foot of the cross—address it head on. Take action in that area today. Maybe you need to repent, maybe you need to call the financial advisor, maybe the doctor. Do one thing to address the lameness, with the intent to heal, so that you may share that healing with others.

Sermon Notes

_____
_____
_____
_____
_____
_____
_____
_____
_____
_____
_____
_____
_____
_____
_____
_____
_____
_____
_____
_____
_____
_____
_____
_____
_____

Filling Cracks

LIKE MANY PEOPLE THESE DAYS, I have bought into the falsehood that I can learn to do anything if I just watch YouTube. I've gone through several periods of "do-it-yourself" obsessive behavior. At one point, I was cutting all of my daughters' hair, and grooming the dog at home—not with the same tools, mind you. Neither the children nor the dog was especially thankful for my efforts, and we've since gone back to the professionals.

Last month, I began to notice the cracks in our shower grout growing longer, deeper, and wider. I also had a hard time getting some of the grout clean and free from mold or mildew. Normally, I don't obsess over my home, but it was January, and cabin fever led me to find problems to address and projects to resolve them. About the same time, my dad mentioned he was regrouting and re-caulking his bathroom shower and tub, so that gave me an idea. I texted him, "Hey, want to do my shower, too?" I was half joking and half hoping he'd leap at the chance to spend time in his retirement on some of my home improvements. I figured he was the perfect one to trust—my father is the handiest of men on the planet. He had built houses, boats, and cars from the ground up. He can fix or engineer anything and if he doesn't know how to do something, he learns everything there is to know, and then does the job beautifully. Unlike me, he was able to do all of his own home repair long before YouTube! I was a bit dismayed at his text response that came shortly afterwards, "There are some great videos on YouTube," complete with a wink emoji. I can take a hint. And who would seriously volunteer to do that job for someone else?

So, I began watching videos on YouTube. Friendly men showed various tools needed for the job and ambitious ladies made the work look so easy. They liked to use words like, "simply," "easily," and phrases like "there you have it." I think one of them even said, "Voila!" After watching several hours of video, I convinced myself I was ready to take on the job and that I had nothing to fear. I ordered all of my tools and supplies on Amazon, and waited to begin my task.

First, I had to remove the old grout, by "simply" running my grout saw along the grout lines and letting the old grout fall away. However, it didn't quite happen that way and the horrible sound from the saw sounded worse than nails on a chalkboard. The saw I ordered was too wide and it started damaging my tile. It took me 45 minutes to reconfigure the grout saw to fit properly. I texted my dad. He said he had a great electric tool I could borrow, so I abandoned my project temporarily, and drove over to his house to get the power tool.

After much instruction from Dad, I returned home and was confident that I would now have success. But I didn't. The sound of the new tool was deafening, and my ears were ringing. The tool was heavy and vibrating so hard that I had trouble controlling the blade and keeping it from ripping my tile apart. And did I mention that the dust and debris were coating every inch of me, my hair, and the bathroom? I was making a big mess, and it was beginning to dawn on me that I had extended my confidence a bit too far.

When I finally got the old grout out, and set about applying the new grout, I found it to be more manageable. It was a more pleasant job and I felt like I was making significant progress until I found more cracks. The more I looked, the more I found. Even the cracks had cracks! As I continued to make a mess, the smell of the new grout was making me sick to my stomach. I was consumed with thinking, "What had I done? Why did I start this? Who did I think I was?"

I finally finished the grout and set to finish the caulking. Armed with the loaded caulk gun, I attempted to run a nice bead of caulk in each corner. But the caulk began pouring out of the gun and dripped everywhere. The silicone was making me lightheaded and I wanted to throw up. All I wanted to do was finish, and I kept making a bigger mess at every turn.

So often, we set out on our own life improvement projects only to end up with failed attempts and still-broken selves. We run from YouTube, to books, to friends, and back to the world, for quick fixes. And like me, standing barefoot and filthy in my shower stall, we stand in our mess, feeling weak and incapable. This is where our heavenly Father steps in, and says:

> *My grace is sufficient for you, my power is made perfect in your weakness.*
>
> *2 Corinthians 12:9*

And when we cry out wondering who we are, Psalm 138:3 (NKJV) says:

> *In the day when I cried out, You answered me, and made me bold with strength in my soul.*

And when we shake in our boots, Psalm 16:8 (NIV) says:

> *I keep my eyes always on the LORD. With Him at my right hand, I will not be shaken.*

It's ok to be weak! We're not meant to be experts at this life, we're meant to let God step in and fill the cracks. The beautiful thing about God is that He says, "It's ok, child. You tried, don't feel so bad, I love you no matter what."

> **We're not meant to be experts at this life, we're meant to let God step in and fill the cracks.**

I'm grateful to have an earthly dad who thinks and acts the same way toward me. My dad has given me glimpses of the way God feels towards His children. I'm so very thankful he shows he is proud of me, even when my attempts at life and home improvement are less than stellar. I'm so very thankful for a kind and loving God who loves me just as I am and doesn't expect me to get it all right.

Address the Mess:

Is there an improvement project in your life you've made into a bigger mess than when you started? Whether it's home improvement, self-improvement, or perhaps a relationship, have you asked God to take the lead on the project? Do that now. Stop trying to DIY your life and your relationships, and surrender your needs over to Jesus.

Sermon Notes

_____

_____

_____

_____

_____

_____

_____

_____

_____

_____

_____

_____

_____

_____

_____

_____

_____

_____

_____

_____

_____

_____

_____

_____

_____

Response in Progress

IF YOU'RE AN iPHONE USER, you likely know about what I call the "dot dot dot" in the text function. It's the little text cloud that appears with an ellipsis in it, when the person you're texting is responding to you. I don't know about you, but I watch the "dot dot dot." If I send a text, I immediately watch to see if the person is writing back. If I see the "dot dot dot," I can't move on to anything else until that text comes through. It's a little obsessive, I know. And oh my gosh, if I see the "dot dot dot" and then no text ever comes through, then I really drive myself crazy wondering about the response that was in progress at one time.

The "dot dot dot" is really called an ellipsis. It's origin, in grammar and mechanics, is used to omit words to consolidate a thought or statement. In more modern writing, it's sometimes used to indicate a pause for thought. And in current instant messaging technology, it's used as a symbol for a response in progress. I admit, I obsess over that little symbol and wait upon a response. Somehow, there's satisfaction in knowing someone is actively responding even if you don't see their response yet.

There are many scriptures that confirm that God waits to hear from us and that He thinks thoughts towards us and answers our prayers (Jeremiah 20:11 is one of them). However, sometimes it seems that God is silent and He doesn't respond. It's as though there wouldn't even be a "dot dot dot" if we had Him on our iPhone. Some people say it feels like their prayers are hitting the ceiling.

The last book of the Old Testament is Malachi. The name Malachi means, "messenger." God's Word through Malachi went out and then there was silence. The book of Malachi was the last prophetic word given to man before the coming of Jesus Christ, and there were 400 years of silence from the Lord in that time period in between. I'm certain God's people were praying and seeking Him, but it's as if that ellipses wasn't even appearing on the screen. The texts went out, but nothing. The prayers went out and nothing seemed to change. No confirmation of receipt or a response in progress. At some point I imagine the people of God putting their phones, or maybe their prayers and hopes, back in their pockets and going about their business. Was God waiting on them in return?

We have no account of that 400 years in the Bible. Maybe people were losing faith. Maybe they began praying less because they weren't getting immediate feedback and response. Maybe their hearts were growing more desperate for the messiah. Were they expectant, hopeful, or anxious, and despondent? I know when someone doesn't write me back, I start to feel ignored. Again, a little obsessive I know, but in our age of instant communication it's normal to expect responses. In the age of prophecy, it was common for God's people to hear from leaders in the community. But now, there was silence, a shrug of the shoulders and maybe those seeking and listening for the Word were saying, "I got nothin'."

That didn't mean the Word was not forthcoming. Jesus was still on His way. God still had a plan. Redemption was near and frankly, 400 years isn't a long time to God, because the Bible says that for God 1000 years is just like a day (Psalm 90:4). The lesson here is that supposed silence from our Lord is only supposed. He is working and active and setting a plan into motion no matter how deafening the silence may seem to us.

Current events might cause us to believe there is nothing but silence on God's part. During that 400 years of biblical silence, the Roman Empire was growing and began saber rattling and the noose was tightening around the Jewish community. Today, we see heinous crimes against Christians and Jews, people of all colors, and hate crimes and lawlessness featured on every newscast. We pray but maybe our prayers grow weaker because we don't see the response in progress. Sometimes there seems to be no indication He's preparing any response at all.

These are the times when the power of faith shows itself. We have the luxury of the completed cannon of scripture. We know what happens after a period of 400 years of waiting. God came in the form of a baby to the world to eventually level the ground at the cross so that all could know God. We now have assurance that all wrongs will be made right and someday, there will be no more tears (Revelation 21:4). We can have faith because He's faithful. That doesn't change no matter what else does around us. And while we faithfully wait, for the response, there's something else we can do.

God also tells the people in the book of Malachi to take a look at mess they've made of their lives, turn it around, and get ready for the coming of something new (Malachi 4). That's pretty convicting and timely. There are messes everywhere. Thankfully, God sent His Holy Spirit to be our Helper after Jesus left this world. We don't have to suffer in silence because we have a living and active Holy Spirit (John 14:16). We have a Savior in Heaven who sits at the right hand of God making intercession for those who call upon Him (Romans 8:34).

Instead of shrugging our shoulders, let us be expectant. He says the "sun of righteousness will rise with healing in its wings" (Malachi 4:2 NIV). Get ready. Clean up the mess. That's a pretty amazing response in progress.

Address the Mess:

On a road trip down a regular highway, the time might seem to pass slowly if all you do is stare out the window at unchanging landscape. However, if the landscape isn't so boring and changes frequently, or if you busy yourself with a good book or game, you will likely be more captivated and engaged, and the time will seem to pass quicker. What our eyes see, and how engaged we are, has a great impact on our perception of time when we are waiting.

Knowing this, take the time to purposely engage yourself while you wait. If you have been praying for something or asking God to reveal His plan, and have not received a response, consider this strategy. Instead of repeating your question, ask God to show you what you can be doing while you wait. Who could you bless while you wait for your blessing? It doesn't make sense to sit still while we wait, make use of that time. Can you be certain that God isn't waiting on you to act in another way? Put your prayer life into action and don't allow excuses for idleness, or despondency in the waiting.

Sermon Notes

_____

_____

_____

_____

_____

_____

_____

_____

_____

_____

_____

_____

_____

_____

_____

_____

_____

_____

_____

_____

_____

_____

_____

_____

Kneeling Hurts

I GREW UP IN A LITURGICAL PROTESTANT CHURCH where an order of service was strictly followed. We understood that we were to say this, sing that, stand up and sit down, stand again, leave, and find coffee in Styrofoam cups at the end. When I was a kid and visited a Catholic church, I was blown away, finding even more things to say and even more movement. It was there that I discovered kneeling. In between the standing up and sitting down there would be a crouching down, with knees on red velvet kneelers that creaked beneath the weight of those who crouched down. I had never seen kneeling and when I asked about it back at my church the explanation was, "We don't need to do that anymore." I received this response as an odd insinuation that we had graduated out that sort of worship, as if it was beneath us.

In the past 10 years or so, I've come to know more about kneeling. There have been a few times when that's all I could do. I could no longer stand and praise or stand and ask for my needs or sit and be thankful. There have been times when all I could do was be on my knees and either cry with joy or with despair. One thing I've learned, is that kneeling hurts.

About 20 years ago, I had a couple of knee surgeries and part of my patellar tendon was removed and bone was taken away from my tibia. With the uneven surface below my right knee from the surgery, crawling on the floor has become very painful. I have a hard time kneeling or being on that knee

> **In that driveway, the pain of every little stone was imprinted into my knees. There were no red velvet cushions between me and the realities of the world.**

for any length of time. Recently, however, I have found kneeling to be the only proper response or way to approach the Lord. At one point, I found myself crouched down in a gravel driveway seeking guidance and making requests to God that seemed like too much to ask; thanking Him for being altogether lovely and a better God than I deserved. In that driveway, the pain of every little stone was imprinted into my knees. There were no red velvet cushions between me and the realities of the world. As minutes went by, every pebble and bit of grass left an imprint and after my time alone with the Lord, I found it difficult to stand.

I decided to do a little more research to understand kneeling. After a quick search through a Bible database I only came up with the word, "kneel" about six times. A few times kneeling is mentioned as someone approaches Jesus to make a request—a mother requesting healing for a child or a leper requesting healing from a disease. Sometimes kneeling is mentioned in regard to those who mocked Jesus as He hung on the cross. I guess our kneeling could even be seen as a mockery or a manipulation with the wrong heart.

I changed my search to "knees" which yielded more results, with most of them in the Old Testament. Many of the references stated phrases such as, "fell to his knees" or "bowed at the knees." In these circumstances, there was true surrender to the Lord, awe, or thanksgiving. In one powerful instance, Solomon dedicates the temple from his knees:

> *Then he knelt on his knees in the presence of all the assembly of Israel, and spread out his hands toward heaven, and said, "O Lord, God of Israel, there is no God like you, in heaven or on earth, keeping covenant and showing steadfast love to your servants who walk before you with all their heart..."*

> *2 Chronicles 6: 13-14*

I found it interesting that there were more references to kneeling and falling on one's knees in the Old Testament. It reminded me of the previous explanation I received as a teenager, as though I were being told, "Oh, that's Old Testament, we don't do that anymore." In reality, if anything should bring us to our knees it would be the stuff of the New Testament! The redemption, the grace, the love and the ultimate sacrifice of Jesus should cause us to bow, or fall to our knees in awe! But kneeling hurts.

Kneeling requires not only the bending of the knee but the bending of our will. Giving up the right to stand or giving up the right to be right. When we kneel, we pass up the opportunity to have our say or the last word. I don't know about you but that's about the hardest thing I know, (or many times don't know), how to do.

> *Kneeling requires not only the bending of the knee but the bending of our will. Giving up the right to stand or giving up the right to be right.*

My imprinted knees reminded me that surrender is painful but leaves an impression on our hearts and on the heart of God. God was faithful to Jesus to bring Him through the ultimate surrender and raise Him up and out of the blackness of the Earth. That same God is faithful and just do the same for us—whether we find ourselves choosing to bend our knees, or falling from awe and surrender.

Address the Mess:

If you are physically able, try kneeling during your daily prayer time if you don't already. Take note of how this posture feels. If you can't kneel (or if you already do), try another posture or location for your prayer time. Look out a different window, take a prayer walk, raise your hands in praise! Do something different and make prayer something in which you actively participate—not just with words, but with your whole body, even if it's uncomfortable.

Sermon Notes

_____

_____

_____

_____

_____

_____

_____

_____

_____

_____

_____

_____

_____

_____

_____

_____

_____

_____

_____

_____

_____

_____

_____

_____

_____

The Little Things

SOMETIMES WE CAN BE SO FOCUSED ON THE BIG PICTURE of Jesus as God, that we miss the little things that He experienced in His humanity. The other day I was thinking about the crucifixion. Heavy stuff, I know, but sometimes I think about the cross and what Jesus went through. And like most people, I envision the nails in His hands and feet. I imagine the crown of thorns that was pressed firmly into His forehead. I imagine the spear that was plunged deep into His side to make sure the deed was completed. Much of this is so familiar to us from hearing the account multiple times, but today I considered as aspect I hadn't thought of before. It might seem like a "little thing" compared to the weight of the world's sin being placed upon His shoulders, but what about the splinters in His back?

It's estimated Jesus hung on that cross for about three hours before He finally gave His life up. They even placed something underneath His feet so that He wouldn't die quickly so as to prolong His suffering. As I contemplated the excruciating pain, anguish, and utter despair He must have experienced, I thought about how every time He must have struggled against the nails and pushed from His feet to take a breath, the splinters must have grated His already brutally beaten back. They must have felt like knives being placed right into open wounds.

It was a crude cross—not the nicely polished thing we have on the wall of our home. It was course and rough. Like our lives, sometimes it isn't the major events that bring us pain or cause us anxiety and fear, it's the little things. It's the tiny splinters that pierce us as we try to adjust to the big stuff around us. And try as we might, we can't get away from the splinters.

I've got friends going through cancer, the loss of loved ones to suicide, the bittersweet season of empty nests, and the uncertainty of job loss and strained finances. For some of these folks that are facing the big things, it's the little things that seem to wear them down the most. It's the side effects of the cancer meds, the quarrelsome family members who argue over the estate, and the tiresome job interviews that don't seem to lead anywhere. The purpose of Christ's suffering was not only for our eternal security but to bring us hope and security during the trials on Earth, too. He handled both the big and the little things on that cross.

Yet even though I know this to be true, sometimes I still think my splinters are too small to bother God about because He's got way too much going on to be concerned with my little things. Threats of nuclear war, rampant hatred and racism, human trafficking and refugee crises seem way more important and pressing to God than my complaints. I sometimes even pray about my little stuff and then dismiss it, thinking that I shouldn't bother Him. However, when we look back at the cross, there's an important "smaller" part of the story that we should remember.

As Jesus carried that cross up the hill, a man named Simon came along and was made to carry it for Him part of the way. I imagine Simon's back was splintered, too. The weight and pain were likely too much. Ultimately, Simon of Cyrene had to give that cross back to Christ and let Him finish the work. While carrying the cross was no small thing, it's important to remember that Jesus was meant to be part of the entire process of carrying our own crosses. He was meant to be with us for the little steps as well as the big steps; for the nails as well as for the splinters.

Matthew 11:28-30 (NIV) is one of my favorite verses. It says:

Come to me, all you who are weary and burdened, and I will give you rest. Take my yoke upon you and learn from me, for I am gentle and humble in heart, and you will find rest for your souls. For my yoke is easy and my burden is light.

He knew we would be weary, and burdened. He knew that sometimes it wasn't the major crosses, but just the splinters that would be wearing us down. And the best part of all, is that He says, we can come to Him with it all. Because if anyone can relate to the impact of the pain of a small splinter, it is surely the One who took them on against freshly-wounded skin.

I would challenge you today, to remember the splinters; the small representation that Christ handled *all of it* on the cross. Christ's crucifixion was a complete work, not only for salvation but so that we might have an abundant life (John 10:10). He took nails in His hands and feet to usher you to heaven, but He also strained against the burden of the smaller struggles and took the splinters for you, too.

Address the Mess

Pray about the little things today. Don't compare your sufferings or situation with that of the entire world. Simon of Cyrene carried that cross for just a little while and eventually handed it off to the One who could bear it all for Him and for all of us. Be specific to name the little things that are bothering you and don't be ashamed to come to Him exactly as you are.

Sermon Notes

_____

_____

_____

_____

_____

_____

_____

_____

_____

_____

_____

_____

_____

_____

_____

_____

_____

_____

_____

_____

_____

_____

_____

_____

_____

_____

Section 4

Blessed are those that hunger and thirst for righteousness for they shall be satisfied.

Matthew 5:6

Results May Vary

I AM A LITTLE EMBARRASSED TO ADMIT THAT I LOVE INFOMERCIALS. Every now and then I even like to watch those shopping channels. Everything featured is always new and improved, solves so many problems, and claims to change lives! My husband and kids make fun of me when they catch me watching and we all love to join in on the repeated phrases like, "But wait, there's more!" or "If you call now!" The popular disclaimer on weight loss and fitness programs is always, "results may vary."

Sometimes we sit in church or read books and we view the Christian testimony like an infomercial. A person has a problem, they seek a solution, they find Jesus, and all of their problems are solved, and they now have a wonderful, spotless life. Just like that! Not so. Not in my experience.

My husband shared his testimony in front of our church several months ago. I stood by him in support, as he shared his struggles with addiction, the hurts of his past, and how it had damaged our marriage. He shared how he found Christ and overcame addiction and how our marriage was restored. I am so very proud of my man.

Immediately following that moment though, people who are in the middle of their own messes have approached us with questions like, "What worked?" and "How long did it take?" I have looked into their hurting faces and read their desperate emails to realize they are seeking the solutions, the quick fixes, and they need relief.

We respond honestly and share some of the things we learned that worked for us. I learned to be thankful in all things (1 Thessalonians 5:18) and how wives need love and husbands need respect. (I highly suggest Emmerson Eggerichs' book, *Love and Respect*, as a great resource for understanding this.) I began practicing respect even when I didn't feel like it (Ephesians 5). Even when I was the most hurt and angry, I sought to serve my husband daily. I began doing little things like making his breakfast and sitting with him before he went off to work. After several weeks of doing this, my heart softened toward him, and his, to mine. He began to do things for me, loving me through service, just like Jesus washing the disciples' feet (John 13).

My husband had his own journey. He attended 12 step programs and support groups. He sought counsel from pastors and godly men. He began serving within the church and singing in our church choir. He found that worship was very healing to him. These are all things that worked for us as individuals and as a couple, but I must add a disclaimer: results may vary.

On the day we shared our story publicly, we didn't have time of course, to share the entire picture of the healing process. We didn't get to share that the years following my husband finding Christ and the start of his healing, were as hard, and almost worse than the years prior. While he was finding Jesus, I was unearthing years of rage, resentment, and regret for not acting sooner. We were raising our three young children on little to no sleep and many tears. We were often not on the same page and struggled to find balance and unity. While I was happy for him, I was often feeling sorry for myself. I still went about doing all things I mentioned before, no matter how I felt, but it wasn't pretty.

If there was small print at the bottom of testimonies it would be this: even when we do the Christ-like things in our relationships like gratitude, forgiveness, and selfless service, the cheaters may still cheat, drinkers may still drink, and the liars may continue to lie. The things we do are meant to bring about change in our own hearts first. What happens with the other person is between them and Lord. Individual results may vary.

That sounds a little discouraging ... but wait, there's more! There is one thing I can guarantee. Jesus promised eternal life to anyone who put complete and total trust in Him. No strings attached and no additional hidden fees or payments. So, while your situation looks grim or that person in your life continues to hurt you, you can at least be guaranteed that when you leave this world there will be no more tears.

Revelation 21:4 says:

> *He will wipe away every tear from their eyes, and death shall be no more, neither shall there be mourning, nor crying, nor pain anymore, for the former things have passed away.*

While the problems of this world seem never ending, they are temporary. We have no way of knowing when our situations will change or when, and if, the people who hurt us will repent but we do have a blessed assurance.

I can't make guarantees that what worked for my husband and me will work for you in your situation. I can make the guarantee that if you call on the Lord and come near to Him, He will come near to you (James 4:8). If you believe in Him, He personally guarantees you an eternity of peace. The best part is there is no money back guarantee because by His grace, it's all free.

Address the Mess:

Hidden sin hurts the one hiding it and ends up having a rippling effect on all of those around them as well. It is impossible to contain the damages, and the Bible says that all things will be brought to light (Luke 8:17), so it is only a matter of time before you will be forced to deal with an issue currently hidden. If these words are at all moving something inside of you, do not turn the page and ignore this. God has brought you to this very moment to allow me to tell you its ok to come right into His light and receive His love and His grace. Memorialize this very day as your stopping point. Confess what needs to be confessed. Repent (turn from) that sin and declare that it will be no more a part of your life. Set up accountability partners who will support and check on you. It was not an accident that you read this page today.

Sermon Notes

You Brood of Vipers

You brood of vipers, how can you who are evil say anything good? For the mouth speaks what the heart is full of.

Matthew 12:34 (NIV)

I MAGINE IF YOU HAPPENED UPON A REAL HEAP OF VIPERS. You wouldn't stand there and debate about whether or not they were poisonous and harmful. You wouldn't wait it out and hope the vipers would turn from their poisonous ways. You would declare to everyone around you, "Watch out! You're going to be hurt if you go any further! Stay away from this, it's dangerous!"

I admit I was a little uncomfortable writing this entry. I don't like confrontation and I would much rather keep the peace in most circumstances. Then God reminded me that I like to sugar coat things, so as not to have to deal with reality. Ouch.

Matthew 12:34 are the very words of Jesus Christ, Himself. He was responding to the Pharisees, whom He called hypocrites. The Pharisees were the ultra-religious ruling class who enslaved their followers with rules and regulations and made them buy their forgiveness with heavy fees. Jesus spoke these words as the Pharisees were trying to entrap Him and force Him into blasphemy. I'm angry about what they were trying to do to Jesus, and yet still slightly uncomfortable with His response. Every time I read

107

Jesus's reply, I want to tap Him on His holy shoulder and whisper, "Um, Jesus, remember what our moms said? 'If you don't have anything nice to say, don't say anything at all.'" I imagine if I were to do this, He might offer me a few choice words, too.

Sometimes the Christian life feels like a great big paradox. We are taught to "turn the other cheek," "pray for our enemies," and "lay down our lives for one another." Like me in this example, we confuse being "nice" with being Biblical. So, when we are wronged, and we burn with anger and hurt, we often drown ourselves in guilt, sometimes over-extending grace to the point where it's not even grace anymore, but misplaced boundaries.

While we can't control what anyone else does, we can control how we participate with it. When we allow another's sin to continue to harm us, we are the foolish ones to not recognize the danger right in front of us and flee from it appropriately. It's like staying in the pit with the vipers. Perhaps Jesus used these strong words to show us it's ok to call things out for what they really are. He was speaking truth. If anyone knew, surely Jesus knew just how dangerous these people really were and He wanted everyone to hear it so they would be protected from the so-called abundant life they were being made to live. We should be so wise to speak truth boldly, especially when the danger is obvious.

I remember a time in my life when I had to call out and name something very harmful in order for my family's life to improve. I had to say the words, "You are an addict" to someone I loved dearly. Oh, those words still sting to this day, because my flesh still soaks in pride. If I'm not careful, shame and embarrassment follow close behind. Yet, if I had not declared the truth, only God knows where my family might be today. We need to follow Jesus's example and call out those things that endanger us, our loved ones, and even our country. Freedom comes when we make our minds up about the things that pose a clear threat to our well-being and then act accordingly.

Of course, we don't seek to publicly shame people, and calling down hellfire and brimstone upon them. But what if instead of making excuses and looking the other way in the face of obvious sin, we called things as they are and distance ourselves appropriately? Yes, "love believes the best" but

Jesus also tells us to pick up our mats and walk, not to be door mats. Naming and then distancing ourselves from obvious danger is not un-Christian-like. This verse is a perfect example of that. Jesus called out the Pharisees because they were getting in the way of people who desperately wanted to

> **Remember, Jesus died for all, even for those Pharisees. He called them what they were, and continued toward the cross for them anyway.**

know God once and for all. We can still separate, pray for the person and the situation, and trust God to do whatever is in His will. Remember, Jesus died for all, even for those Pharisees. He called them what they were, and continued toward the cross for them anyway.

Address the Mess:

What, or who, is getting in the way of the abundant life Jesus died for you to have? Name it. This is not judgment and it definitely is not an excuse for hypocrisy. Look clearly at yourself so that you can look clearly at your brother or sister (Matt 7:1-5). When you are sure of the obvious danger, look to the Bible to see specifics as to how to deal with that particular sin, and then do just that. Don't do the thing that makes you comfortable. Confront it. Be prayerful and make some changes.

Sermon Notes

_____
_____
_____
_____
_____
_____
_____
_____
_____
_____
_____
_____
_____
_____
_____
_____
_____
_____
_____
_____
_____
_____
_____
_____
_____

Lip Wax and God's Honest Truth

I LOVE THE LADY WHO DOES MY NAILS, her name is Mary. I go through little spurts of keeping my nails freshly painted. (It's one of those niceties a girl needs sometimes.) Even if my hair is a mess and there's no make-up on my face, it makes me feel good when my nails look nice.

One day, while enjoying this luxury, I sank into the chair across from Mary and stretched out my hands in full surrender for her to buff and polish. A little out of the ordinary, Mary looks up and deep into my eyes. She scans my face and I look back at her smiling, but a little uncomfortable. Maybe there's something in my nose? Maybe I have bad breath? She looks me over once more and says, "You want your lip waxed today?" *Gee thanks, Mary.*

I sheepishly reply, "No, thanks, I don't need it." Now I'm red and want to crawl out of the chair and hope that none of the ladies at the other chairs heard our exchange. (Men, if you're reading, you do not speak of this to me, or the women in your life...ever.)

"Yes, you do. It will only take a minute," she insists. As soon as my nails dry, she asks me to follow her to the back room. There, I lie on the table as she applies hot wax to my lip and eyebrows and wherever else she finds unsightly hairs. I'm so embarrassed, but secretly thankful Mary was helping me. She's the tiniest little lady, so it's a little startling that she doesn't often take no for an answer.

She finishes and says I look much better now and sends me off. I don't even know what I tipped her because I didn't want anyone to see my glowing red face as I hurriedly left the salon.

What's all this got to do with Jesus? I am reminded that God's Word is often compared to a mirror. We may find the Bible to be offensive at times, because in it, we see ourselves and our shortcomings. When we read things like, "love your enemy," "be anxious for nothing," "submit to one another," and "be slow to speak and slow to anger" we may recoil. Just like I wish Mary would accept my pre-menopausal upper lip, I wish God would just let me remain as I am. I want to stay obstinate, worrisome, and I want to have my right to complain and hate. But God says, "No, you've got a little something we need to take care of and I'm going to help you with it."

Thankfully, God is gentle and merciful in His restoration. God provided His only son as a perfect example of how to live and knows that we can't meet that standard on our own. Romans 5:8 says "but God shows his love for us in that while we were still sinners, Christ died for us." God has given us His Word so that we may know His love and learn to live like His son. Yes, He calls His Word a sword, but it's not meant to

> *The Lord is just like that... not condemning but caring and wanting to see His child at her best. So instead of avoiding Him and His word, it's worth a sit-down with hands extended in full surrender to allow Him to polish and refine us.*

shred and shame you, only to cut away the ungodly, polish and refine you, and keep you looking like His best.

I sometimes let myself go. I let the nail polish chip and I avoid Mary because I know she won't let me get away until I'm as beautiful as she'd like me to be. But when I sit with her, she asks about my children and my husband. She tells me she loves the polish I chose and how nice it will go with my clothes. She likes to see me at my best. The Lord is just like that...not condemning but caring and wanting to see His child at her best. So instead of avoiding Him and His word, it's worth a sit-down with hands extended in full surrender to allow Him to polish and refine us.

Address the Mess:

Memorize God's Word:

> *I have loved you with an everlasting love;*
> *therefore, I have continued my faithfulness to you.*

> *Jeremiah 31:3*

Now, knowing that God loves you, ask Him to show you what needs to be cleaned up in your life. Your language? Your giving? Your trust issues? The way you treat your spouse, your kids? Name what needs to be removed and ask God to come alongside you to help you. Maybe you already went through something like this but like those pesky lip hairs (i.e. your sin problem) returned. Finally, tell someone what you're working on, whether it's an online friend or co-worker. Someone who will hold you accountable and call you out like my Mary does when I don't show up looking like my best.

Sermon Notes

Shut the Front Door

I LIVE ON A CUTE CUL-DE-SAC IN A PRETTY TYPICAL SUBDIVISION. My home is on the corner of the cul-de-sac and busy street and our neighborhood is full of kids. When my kids were little, my front door was left open all day to welcome in kids and other moms. Anyone could walk by and peer into the window of our lives. Sometimes while kids were riding bikes or playing kick ball, moms would stop in to chat and commiserate about life with kids and busy husbands.

One day all of this changed for me. On September 30, 2008, I shut the front door. On that day, my family went into crisis mode and I instinctively shut my door to the outside world. I'm not talking about total isolation. I would describe it as insulation. Instead of calling 911 on a desperate situation, I hit my knees and cried out to God and then a very select few people including family, friends and pastors.

What I knew deep down was that there were folks who would have reveled in my disaster. I needed people who would maintain confidentiality and secure our dignity. I believe now without those two things we would not have survived. It was a time when I had to reevaluate everything from friends to finances, and rein in my life. I needed people around me who would pray and not publish.

Please don't misunderstand, I have amazing neighbors. In the weeks following our stuff hitting the fan, kind neighborhood friends came to my aid to babysit, listen, and share their own struggles. But for a short while,

I needed to hunker down, prioritize and join God in the mission of saving my family.

Maybe you're not in crisis mode but you have this nagging feeling that something's got to change. You have a kid who's not quite right, a spouse who seems disengaged, or you have some holes in your heart that need mending. Don't wait like I did to shut the front door. If I'm honest, I chose the distractions of motherhood, friends, and kids over dealing with the stuff that was gnawing away at our life. I knew deep down something wasn't right in my house, but I was too afraid to deal and face it. There's a reason why God says "fear not" 365 times, we need to "fear not" every day of the year.

On the flip side, if you have a friend who has recently dropped out of life, it might be time to check in with him or her. The mom who is a play date dropout, or the guy who doesn't show up for the regularly scheduled golf outing

> *Don't assume someone is being rude, anti-social or busy. They might be crying too hard to cry for help.*

could be in crisis mode but too fearful to tell you. I dealt with unbearable amounts of embarrassment and shame. I quickly learned that my real friends were the ones who kindly checked in with me and asked that loaded question, "Are you okay?" Don't assume someone is being rude, anti-social or busy. They might be crying too hard to cry for help.

It's been over a decade now and so much healing has gone by since that dreadful day. God has done a new thing in my family and in my heart. In the past few years, I've been able to open my door to many different people who need hospitality and help. As a couple we have helped families facing addiction, a few moms navigating homeschooling for the first time, and friends at the end of their rope. Shutting the front door isn't forever, it's only as long as it takes for the Lord to work in your life and get you to the place where you can open it again to help others.

Address the Mess:

Are you avoiding handling the tough stuff in your life because you're choosing to be distracted by life? Do you need to refocus and shut your front door so you can deal and heal? Do the hard thing and commit to focusing on the things that really matter. Today is your start day.

Sermon Notes

Free Range Jesus

IN OUR COMMUNITY, A MOTHER AND FATHER HAD RECENTLY BEEN INVESTIGATED and harassed by authorities for allowing their children to walk to and from a park about a mile from their home. The police cited that these children were "playing alone," which is apparently a crime in today's society.

Upon hearing this, I wanted to write about the importance of allowing our kids to go out and get exercise, and that sometimes a little free-roaming isn't so bad. I also considered writing about the overreaches of the "authorities." It's amazing to me that some localities believe they have the right to tell you what you can pack in your kids' lunch or what size soda can be purchased at the movies. But after pondering all of this, I still have mixed sentiments. Sometimes I think the world is dangerous and scary and I wouldn't let my kids walk alone, and sometimes I let them loose to explore and create and be independent. My mind roamed to the story in Luke Chapter 2, when young Jesus is left at the Temple.

In this story, Jesus's parents made a journey to Jerusalem to celebrate Passover and upon their return they realized that twelve-year-old Jesus was not with them. It wasn't a few minutes into the journey when they realized; it was a couple of days later! Now before we call the authorities on Mary and Joseph, we need to recognize that these journeys were taken by large family clans of hundreds of people. Children were likely in the back of the caravan hopping and playing along while the men and animals led the way. So, it wasn't like Jesus would have just been in the back seat of the minivan listening to his tunes.

Imagine of the horror of realizing your kid isn't with you. The highways of Bible times were dangerous, complete with thieves and bandits. Mary and Joseph immediately turned around to make the three-day journey back, only to find Jesus teaching in the Temple. The twelve-year-old was teaching the rabbis! The Bible says all were amazed at His wisdom and understanding. We have the luxury of knowing that they were getting front row seats with God, Himself, but the folks of the day just thought they had some Bible protégé kid among them.

Mary and Joseph seem pretty ticked off at their son and even state, "Why are you treating us this way?" I laugh because Luke did not write down, "What on God's green earth were you thinking you little...!?" which is probably what I would have said. And Jesus gives a respectful and truthful response, "Why were you looking for me? Did you not know that I must be in my Father's house?" That must have hit their guts pretty hard. Jesus basically says, "I'm right where I should be. I'm doing what I'm purposed to do. I'm safe and you shouldn't have worried."

God allowed Jesus to hang back so Jesus could begin His teaching ministry. Imagine the wonder on the rabbis' faces when a twelve-year-old boy was able to explain the mysteries of God and His ways. Jesus had to be free to begin fulfilling the purpose God had for Him. And perhaps there's a lesson there with our own children. As parents, we plan and schedule and make a path for our kids. Sometimes when they get lost, or don't fit the vision we have for them, we become indignant and we think or sometimes say, "Why are you doing this to us?" And our kids, who might not realize that God is working in their lives, feel pulled and confused and don't even know why they're off track. Perhaps by being off track, even in the unsavory things, they are working out God's plan.

It's hard to believe addiction and rehab might be part of God's plan, but what if your kid is supposed to help others from the grips of addiction? It might seem the talent they have abandoned means dollars and hours lost, but what if they can now use those dollars and hours to minister to someone else instead of focusing on themselves? Maybe your kid isn't meant to be a straight A student, perhaps college isn't even where he or she should end up. Are we confident in God's love and care of our children to let them "free range" a bit?

We ought to be thankful for our free-range Jesus. If He hadn't begun His ministry of going about and forgiving and loving and healing, I'm not sure where our world would be today. Even the very "best" guys of Jesus's day weren't very good at maintaining an example. Jesus's path was so radical and so against the establishment it eventually brought Him death. As parents, we fear death and persecution for our kids. I don't believe God wants that for our kids either. But I do believe God wants us to trust Him with our children and allow our kids to explore what His plans are for them.

Address the Mess:

I once had to ask my dear friend if she was idolizing her children. Hearing her great concern for where her kids were at in their walk, I knew that her focus had shifted much more to her children than to Jesus. We can easily make idols out of good things, like ministry or parenting. Hard question: what things do you think about more than Jesus? This is not to shame or condemn you, but to help you understand where your focus is being spent. Not even the most important ministries in our life such as family or marriage should take place over Jesus.

Imagine your mental focus being represented as a pie chart. Consider what categories would be currently be assigned to the chart and do an honest reflection of how much each category takes up. Is Jesus even on the chart, or has He wandered off your radar?

Sermon Notes

_____

_____

_____

_____

_____

_____

_____

_____

_____

_____

_____

_____

_____

_____

_____

_____

_____

_____

_____

_____

_____

_____

_____

_____

_____

Section 5

Blessed are the merciful for they shall receive mercy.

Matthew 5:7

And Then I Slapped Her

AS A KID, I NEVER GOT TO GO TO OVERNIGHT SUMMER CAMP but during the summers while I was in elementary school, I went to day camp at a local community center. It was down the street from the store where my mom worked. I guess she knew it was wise to keep me in close proximity.

The last summer of camp though, I thought I was too old for the little kid camp. I made better friends with the camp counselors than I did with the other campers, because frankly, I was significantly more mature. I spent more time hanging out with the counselors and they seemed to like spending time with me as well. I got all kinds of special privileges.

There were also three girls who hated me, though. They made it very clear and somehow, we always got stuck at the same table doing crafts and whatever busy-work we were given. They used to make fun of me all the time and tell me to shut up. The counselors kept telling me not to worry about them and to ignore them.

One day after kickball, we sat down in the air conditioning to paint. The three girls laughed amongst themselves and made sure to make me feel excluded. I tried to join the conversation and their leader told me to shut up again. So, I stood up. And she stood up. And then I slapped her.

I hit her hard and I left a mark. The room got silent and the counselors who watched it happen covered their snickers and giggles. The sweaty girl turned red and her friends didn't know what to do. I left the table and ate my lunch with the counselors. I didn't even get in trouble because I was one of their favorites.

Let's be honest. It wasn't right. Even though they were like a little pack of mean-girl bullies, it wasn't right because I knew better. My family raised me to never hit anyone in anger. It also wasn't right because I knew I'd get away with it, because I was the counselors' favorite.

Somehow, this makes me think of the Church. Sometimes I think Christians go around thinking they are God's favorites and they can slap people around. Many like to use social media as a way to insult, berate and belittle those who they think are wrong. Many hide behind blogs and would never say the hateful things to someone's face.

Who are we to think we have it all right and that we are to bring about judgement to everyone we meet? It's not a healthy witness to the world when we act as though we are the "favorites" and can get away with bad behavior. Remember, "all have sinned and fall short of the glory of God" (Romans 3:23). "All" means you, and me, and everyone. How about we simply share the love we've found in our relationship with Jesus Christ and meet some needs? Perhaps someone would ask and listen to your point of view on today's state of affairs if you weren't slapping them in public.

Yes, there's a place and time to be the alternative voice. But God's word says in Proverbs 16:24 (NIV), "Gracious words are a honeycomb, sweet to the soul and healing to the bones." What's the motivation behind your rant? Is it to save souls and heal bones or is it just to be right?

Address the Mess:

Sometimes we call out the brood of vipers appropriately to warn others of obvious danger, and sometimes we speak gracious words, where love covers a multitude of sin. We need Holy Spirit discernment to know the appropriate time and place for each. The position of our heart makes all the difference as to whether we are sinful or Biblical in our actions. When have you used your words to cut and wound instead of heal? Think of the most recent occurrence. Confess the sin of using your tongue to wound. Confess to

God and ask for forgiveness from the person you wounded. Take the time to call, write to or see the person you wounded. Acknowledge how you hurt them, and ask for forgiveness without justifying your behavior or anger.

If you used social media to hurt or wound someone, use your platform to publicly apologize. If you find yourself using social media to bicker and criticize, fast from it for a week. Take social media off of your phone and tablet. Assess how much time you spend there and how you use social media. If you find you are always being critical or debating, unfriend or unfollow the people or pages where you are constantly critical. If you can't resist, perhaps you need to be away from social media altogether. Flee from things that pose even a personal danger towards sin for you.

Sermon Notes

_____

_____

_____

_____

_____

_____

_____

_____

_____

_____

_____

_____

_____

_____

_____

_____

_____

_____

_____

_____

_____

_____

_____

_____

_____

_____

_____

_____

Our Hearts, God's Heart

A S A MOM, I SOMETIMES STRUGGLE BETWEEN TOUGH AND TENDER LOVE. I strive not to be the hovering helicopter parent that gets a bad rap for coddling and protecting her children. But lately, I've learned to press into that love for my children a little bit harder because it helps me to understand the love my Father in heaven has for me, just a little bit more.

I grew up in church and Sunday school and knew that Jesus loved me from a very young age, but honestly, up until the last few years I didn't understand how deep and how wide that love was. I didn't understand how fierce and how raw and how gentle and tender God's heart really is.

Many of my friends have had major life changing moments with their kids. Some have undergone severe illnesses and risky surgeries; some have sent their children off to college or the military, and some sit awake night after night praying for their child's health or wellbeing. I sent my older kids off to church camp once for a week and was surprised at myself as I drove home in the car with tears stinging my eyes. I was praying that they would be safe, be kind to someone who needed a friend and learn to love the Lord just a little bit more. If summer camp brought that much emotion to my heart, I can only imagine what college, marriage, grand-children and all the rest will do to me. (Begin praying for my sweet husband now.)

But what God has revealed to me in all of this, is that His Word is not full of trite, small answers to life. While some of it looks great on a coffee mug or framed artwork in the sitting room, Scripture is really the revelation of His heart for us, as a parent. Two examples that particularly strike me include Jeremiah 31:3:

> ...the Lord appeared to him from far away. I have loved you with an everlasting love; therefore I have continued my faithfulness to you.

and Exodus 34:14:

> For you must not worship any other god, for the Lord, whose name is Jealous, is a jealous God.

God's love is eternal, immense and intense. Yet, I misunderstood that Exodus verse for a long time. I saw that word jealous and I could only think of the jealous and emotionally abusive boyfriend who controlled me as a teen. That word jealous kept me from wanting to know the Lord too closely because perhaps, He would turn out to be controlling and belittling to me. As a parent of three beautiful girls, I now know that word "jealous" points to the protective, "Mama Bear" care I have for my girls. I would fight tooth and nail and climb over any obstacle to keep them from harm or destruction. And if I feel this way in my heart, how much more did Jesus feel, as he climbed the hill to Calvary with a cross on His back to die for the entire world's sin? Can you even fathom? I cannot.

So as we parents send our kids off down the hall for the surgery, down the road to boot camp, or out for their first date, we say and pray things like:
"Be Safe!"
"Come back to me whole and in one piece!"
"Make good choices and be a good friend!"
"Remember everything I taught you!"
"Don't believe the lies of the world!"
and
"Remember that I love you the most!"

Without even knowing it, we are speaking the heart of God to our children.

And rend your heart and not your garments "Now return to the LORD your God, For He is gracious and compassionate, slow to anger, abounding in loving kindness and relenting of evil.

Joel 2:13

He has told you, O man, what is good; and what does the Lord require of you but to do justice, and to love kindness, and to walk humbly with your God?

Micah 6:8

The LORD your God is in your midst, a mighty one who will save; he will rejoice over you with gladness; he will quiet you by his love; he will exult over you with loud singing.

Zephaniah 3:17

It's impossible to fully understand how much our God loves us. Parenting has given me a glimpse of His heart. I pray my children have seen Him through me.

Address the Mess:

If you are a parent, I want you to schedule a day to rest. Create your own Mothers or Father's Day. Maybe it's on a day when the kids are not at home, or maybe you create a few hours of space for yourself when they are home. Do something for yourself and take time to reflect on the goodness that you are not alone in your parenting. The Lord your God is with you.

If you are not a parent, take a moment to consider the good that your parents have done for you, regardless of your current relationship with them. Consider the specific attributes in them that have been used to shape you for the better. If you are able, send them a text or make a phone call to thank them, or God for the work He's done in specifically choosing them to be used in your life.

Sermon Notes

Mike Rowe, Dirty Jobs, and Jesus

MY FAMILY HAS ALWAYS ENJOYED American talk show host, Mike Rowe. Mike is known for his shows, "Dirty Jobs" and "Somebody's Gotta Do It" on CNN and the Discovery Channels. We also enjoy listening to him narrate the show "Deadliest Catch." There's something very humble and likeable about Mike that I think most Americans can enjoy. He seems to be able to talk with just about anyone! It's always fascinating to me to watch him step into and explore jobs that nobody else wants to do. Mike brings a good perspective to us all that indeed there are people doing these types of "unwanted" jobs on a regular basis.

Many episodes involve Mike in precarious situations with animals and the messes they make. Sometimes he crawls inside large machines to fix or maintain them. Then there are the shows where he is hands-on with something like wastewater management, literally having to swim and make way through human waste to handle equipment. It's unthinkable that with all of our technology, there are still aspects of this process that require hands-on involvement like this. And yet, there are people who regularly do these unthinkable jobs.

The producers of the show are obviously seeking assignments for Mike that would be memorable to the audience. And Mike, humble as he is, is willing to go right into the thick of it, to show the rest of us, a fresh new perspective on the conditions in which others live and work. The Bible gives us a similar picture of a man who did this, with much greater impact.

Jesus walked through communities, facing the worst of the worst, hands-on. One of my favorite examples deals with the demon possessed man, found in Mark, chapter 5. The picture of this guy is nothing short of memorable. He is a resident of the graveyard —literally living among the tombs. He is naked and is torturing himself by cutting his skin with the sharp edges of stones and screaming out constantly. No one wanted to go near him because he was not able to be tamed or restrained. He was a danger to himself and any others around him. He was everything we would tell our kids to stay away from. If we're honest, he's somebody most of us adults would stay away from, also.

And yet even in his lowly, outcast condition, the Bible says that Jesus takes the time to engage with him. Seeing he is clearly being tormented, Jesus goes right into the dirtiest part of the situation and speaks directly to the demons, named "Legion," who had possessed him. I find it quite interesting when Jesus seeks information, that clearly, He already has access to, as God. Perhaps He simply wanted to provide us a model for how attentive and purposeful we can be even in the dirtiest and lowliest conditions.

After speaking to the demons, Jesus casts them into a herd of two thousand pigs who hurl themselves off a cliff into the ocean. Weird, right? All who saw were amazed and the man got up, freed from his legion, got dressed and proclaimed a victorious new life. What a spectacle. That was a dirty job no one wanted to do. Christ came along and faced it, head on.

When is the last time we saw someone desperately hurting and went to ask them their name? When is the last time we took the time to engage with someone as outcast from society as this man? I'm often too scared to confront a friend deep in sin, or the homeless woman at the fast food restaurant cursing loudly, let alone asking for some stranger's name so I could pray for them. What vast wisdom we can learn by watching episodes of our Master at work!

There are several other messy examples in the Bible of Jesus tackling dirty, unwanted jobs. Many include healing physical ailments of people that were shunned from their communities and environments because of their conditions. Sometimes Christ even literally got down in the dirt, Himself, by spitting and making mud to heal a blind man's eyes. Again, weird! There's so much speculation about why He used the spit and the mud. Yet maybe a better question to ask here would be, "Why does the God of the universe need to use any tools to heal?" Maybe it's as simple as Him showing us that He was willing to get dirty for our sakes.

> *Why does the God of the universe need to use any tools to heal?" Maybe it's as simple as Him showing us that He was willing to get dirty for our sakes.*

Finally, the night of His arrest, Jesus finds Himself in a "Somebody's Gotta Do It" situation. While there is some speculation about what He was asking of His Father (depending on which theologian you ask), I personally believe His prayer is a double check to ask the Father if there's any other way other than the horror of the cross. I believe that in all of His humanity, that Jesus did exactly what we would do if confronted with a brutal, heart-wrenching, unthinkable task. We would ask if there was another way.

Thankfully, He yielded to His Father's will and took up His cross and endured the bloodied knees, welts on his back, spikes in his wrists and feet, and thorns dug deeply into His temples. The scene was so ugly, disgraceful, and painful but He was willing. He was the only One willing to do a job no one else could do. And He thought of every one of us as He went to the dirtiest, most memorable, most unthinkable job to ever present itself to the human race; the "job" of saving humanity from itself. So very messy.

Address the Mess:

Perhaps instead of watching the episodes and treating them like some spectacle, we need to follow the example, not take ourselves so seriously, and jump in.

While you can't necessarily fix someone's mess entirely on your own, you could look for a friend in need today and engage with them right in their situation. Get your hands dirty with them. Show them you're willing to be there with them even if others aren't. Just for a moment, take an honest look from their perspective to see how their world looks. And then try to show them the presence of the Savior with you both.

Sermon Notes

_____

_____

_____

_____

_____

_____

_____

_____

_____

_____

_____

_____

_____

_____

_____

_____

_____

_____

_____

_____

_____

_____

_____

_____

_____

Half-Priced Tattoos

KIDS MAKE RIDICULOUS CHOICES. I know I've heard something about the decision area of the brain not fully forming until age twenty-five or something like that, but it's pretty frustrating when you've said, "No," "Never," "Not under my roof," and then that very thing happens. Some stuff our kids do is no big deal and some of it makes us stare at the ceiling at night asking God when it is going to stop. I think I gave my parents a couple of these moments.

I was a pretty good kid overall, and my mom describes me as compliant. The truth is, I observed my older sibling and friends and learned how to do the same things they did, just more discreetly. I'm not proud of this and I thank Jesus for coming into my life and forgiving me and making my life beautiful after I tried my best to mar it up. One of my really stupid mistakes was a tattoo. Let me say, I love tattoos and I admire many of my friends' body art, but mine was totally wrong. If you know me, none of this story matches up with my personality at all.

When I was in college, credit card companies set up tables in the student union and gave unprepared 19-year-olds high credit limits and free water bottles. I was one of them; proudly walking around with a brand-new credit card when the opportunity presented itself. I had ventured to the tattoo parlor a few times with friends and thought this would be the very thing to prove that I was an independent thinker, different from my very conservative parents, and cool enough to hang out with the rougher group of college kids. One day at the tattoo shop, I saw what I was sure was a sign that this was a good decision: the half-price wall.

Yes, this shop which catered to the nearby college town, had half priced tattoos. I very wisely turned down any of the cartoon tattoos, because I mean how sexy is Garfield or Snoopy? Instead, I settled in on a lovely little dolphin jumping through a half moon, not because I was an aspiring marine biologist or because a dolphin had once saved me after falling overboard at sea. I still have no idea why I chose it. Maybe because it was the only thing that wasn't dark, disrespectful, or cartoonish. Still having a very healthy fear of my parents who were funding my college education, I chose the ever-popular lower back as the dolphin's new home. It was easy to cover up and also easy to strategically reveal with the right jeans. Ugh.

So here I am over two decades later with a faded "tramp stamp" of an aquatic mammal on my back. I've had to explain it to my kids and deal with the jeers of my mom friends when it peeks out from my waistband. It's pretty amusing really and I'm thankful I didn't charge my way into a much larger design that would be harder to hide.

I'm sure I grieved my mom's heart when she finally discovered my tattoo. It wasn't what she expected of me and I know she hated seeing my body permanently changed. The thing is, she didn't yell at me. She just looked at it and said, "Did it hurt?" I told her that it didn't hurt that badly, and that was it. She didn't shame me or tell me how stupid it was or anything. I think she knew my ridiculous choice was painful enough, and there was no need to pile on more. Even though I got a half-priced tattoo, my mom didn't show me half-priced grace. I'm thankful for my mom's mercy and I'm thankful for God's mercies. I'm now a mom of teens and hope and pray they don't fall for half-priced truth of any sort. And I pray that when they do reveal their mistakes, that I am as merciful and understanding as my mom, and my Heavenly Father.

Address the Mess:

Thinking back on your teens or twenties, what is one thing that you sincerely wish you hadn't done? If there is a younger person in your life, share that truth with them today and give them your perspective on it, now, in hindsight.

Sermon Notes

_____

_____

_____

_____

_____

_____

_____

_____

_____

_____

_____

_____

_____

_____

_____

_____

_____

_____

_____

_____

_____

_____

_____

_____

_____

_____

_____

_____

Never Forget

I DON'T KNOW ABOUT YOU, BUT I HAVE A HARD TIME WITH SEPTEMBER 11TH. Every year when the calendar flips over to September, I hold my breath a little and occupy my mind with other things, trying to pretend it didn't happen. I try not to remember that cool, crisp September morning and how I was getting ready for my surprise baby shower at work that wasn't a surprise. I try to forget the call over the loudspeaker to evacuate my office building right before the baby shower and how I ran to my parking garage with my huge, eight-months-pregnant belly. I try to forget the fear and regret I was having about bringing my first-born child into a world where such violence and hatred existed. And as the remembrance posts begin to show up in my Facebook feed, I scroll past looking for an ad or a meme to help take the pain away.

I saw one of those 9-11 posts the other day that said, "Never Forget." I smirked and thought, "Really, how could I forget? How could anyone forget? What a silly thing to suggest"... but not really. Because I forget every day.

I forget a lot of things. I forget the one item my husband asks me to pick up at the grocery store or the dish I am supposed to bring to the pot-luck meal. I forget to pay a bill or return library books. I forget to have my oil changed and some days I don't remember how old I am. And it doesn't stop there.

When it comes to my faith, I forget the big things. I forget that God has been faithful to His children for thousands of years—faithful to provide and to lead them, even in their wanderings. I forget that God rescues, redeems, and restores. I don't recall the many miracles that He has performed over the course of time or even the miracles in my own life and then I find myself fretful and anxious. I forget the simple commands of loving Him and loving my neighbor and I act snarky, hurtful, and downright mean. When I forget God, I become desperate and fearful and I condemn others and myself.

Yes, we need to be reminded to never forget, and God knows it. He warns His people to "never forget" over and over in the Bible. There are phrases like, "lest you forget," and "you shall not forget." He wants His people to remember His faithfulness, their mistakes, His kindness and their need for Him. He wants us to remember the full payment that was provided for those mistakes. To never forget the love and adoration God showered on this planet the day He sent His one and only. To never forget Jesus's ministry to the outcasts, the poor, the widows and orphans, and the despicable. To never forget how Jesus asked God to forgive the ones who put Him on the cross, which included you, me and everyone—even the ones who hated Him. He wants us to recognize and remember, that the most important thing to ever happen to us, was Him.

Address the Mess:

God says He will remember our sin no more (Heb 8:12). It's not that His memory is literally wiped clean, it is referencing that there is no longer a debt associated with it. Consider it like a credit card statement that comes in the mail and shows your purchases, but the balance says zero; no payment due. God has already paid for you and everything that came along with you. You were purchased at the highest-price ever paid—Jesus. So, if you really believe that, what sin in your past are you still holding a self-imposed balance for? If we are to never forget His sacrifice, then maybe it's time to forget the things that were cancelled out because of it, and stop paying interest on a zero balance.

Sermon Notes

_____

_____

_____

_____

_____

_____

_____

_____

_____

_____

_____

_____

_____

_____

_____

_____

_____

_____

_____

_____

_____

_____

_____

_____

_____

_____

When God Wrote a Check

O NE MORNING BEFORE THE SUN CAME UP, I was scurrying around in the dark, packing snacks and making sure my daughter had all she needed for her early morning swim practice. It was dark and damp and I was dreading the impending rain for our commute to her pool. There was still a chill in the air, so I decided to warm up the car before we set out. I slid into the seat, put the key into the ignition and nothing. Nothing. My car made not even the slightest attempt to start. I was now a bit panicked and tried a couple more times with no success.

I quickly ran up the stairs to wake up my husband, who came down to help us. In the flurry of activity, trying to get my car to start, we ended up with not one, but both of our cars dead. I have no idea of what the odds are that both cars would have unexpectedly died at the same time, but there we were. My fears of my daughter being late or missing swim practice turned into realization and despair. While my husband attempted to jump start my vehicle, my worries were also jump started. I began to imagine the worst... *Now we have to buy two new cars? This is going to sink us; this will be thousands of dollars of repairs.*

What made all of this more discouraging is that we had been on a fast and furious debt reduction for the previous couple of years. Our oldest daughter was about to go to college that fall, and we were diligently slashing expenses, paying off debt, and working to be the most fiscally responsible we had ever been. I'm certain we would have made Dave Ramsey proud! And now, our progress was being threatened with two broken cars that had to

149

be towed from our driveway to be assessed and repaired. I quickly began to look at finances to think of the best way to manage this new expense.

After a couple of days, we learned that my vehicle's total cost of towing, parts, and labor was a thousand dollars. It was not as bad as I had imagined, and certainly not as expensive as replacing the car, but still, a blow to our budget. Conversely, my husband's car only needed a new fuse. He and my dad were able to troubleshoot and repair his vehicle. The cost of the replacement fuse was a mere 10 cents. Yet, this situation threw a wrench in our debt reduction plans by a thousand dollars, and was going to delay our self-imposed debt-free deadline that we were looking forward to.

A few days later, it was the week before Easter, and I was feeling extremely anxious about the situation. Even though our cars were now repaired, and I was thankful the situation was not worse, I was overcome with resentment. I felt resentment for the inconvenience, resentment toward myself for not being in better financial shape by now, and resentment for what felt like, too many broken things. It covered me like a dark cloud, and I started to pace the floor and I prayed, "God, I'm so sorry I feel this way, you have blessed us beyond belief, yet I am so mad right now. What do I need to do to remove this resentment?" The answer came to me very clearly, "Thank Me."

Thanksgiving was to be the cure for my dark feelings. So, I began to count my blessings, the big and the small. I thanked God for meeting our needs, for our health, our home, my husband, my children. I thought of every possible thing to thank Him for and little by little, the darkness faded.

As I prayed, I heard the mail truck making its way up my street. My youngest daughter ran out to the mailbox as she does every day to check for her sweet pen pal's letters. I came downstairs to find the mail on the island in the kitchen—mostly junk mail, but also a hand-written envelope addressed to me that caught my attention. There was no return address and it was postmarked from Harrisburg, Pennsylvania, which was odd, as I don't know anyone there. I opened the envelope expecting some advertising scheme inside, only to find a United States money order made out to me for $1000 from none other than "God." My heart pounded. I scanned the cashier's check over and over—could this be real? I even googled the post office code on the check, and this was indeed a legitimate check.

I quickly took the check down to my husband's office and placed it on his desk. He just stared in disbelief. We had heard plenty of messages in church about people receiving unexpected gifts from the Lord, but it always seemed to happen to someone else. We cried in awe and thanksgiving. We felt undeserving of such kindness; it was truly humbling. My husband asked me who could have done it, and while I had some ideas, I only knew one thing for sure. God had made it clear to me, that He is ultimately our provider. Every good and perfect gift is from Him (James 1:17). God inspired someone's generosity and they obeyed. It's as simple as that.

That evening, as we sat watching tv, my husband looked at me and said with wonder, "God wrote us a check today." I chuckled and agreed, "Yes, He did." We just shook our heads and smiled. There I was, panicked, worried, and resentful, and God showed His loving kindness, even when I took my eyes off Him. I am no believer in the prosperity gospel often preached from tele-evangelists but I do believe that my God will supply all my needs according to His riches (Phil 4:19).

We all have a need greater than groceries and car repairs. We have a need for our sins to be covered, paid for, and redeemed. We remember the day that Jesus Christ hung on a cross to die a death that would erase the sins for all who trust in Him. He died for all. He covers the sin and the shame of all. His death redeems all. When Christ gave up His spirit, He uttered, "It is finished." This language is the same language used in a financial transaction; Jesus was canceling the debt of our sin. On Good Friday, Jesus wrote a check to wipe away every debt noted on our accounts. And one year, right before Easter, I received a literal check as a reminder.

Address the Mess:

How can you send a surprise anonymous blessing this week? I still don't know who sent that money but someone went to the post office and mailed that money order. What could you do? You don't have to give a thousand dollars to deeply impact someone's life. Perhaps you pay for someone's meal across the restaurant or the car behind you in the drive thru. Maybe you go to the town office and settle someone's delinquent water bill for them. If you can't afford a financial blessing, send someone a card telling them how much they are loved and cherished by God. Have fun with this one. Ministry can be a hoot! Imagine the person's face when they receive their blessing. Praise God for getting to be a part of it!

Sermon Notes

Section 6

Blessed are the pure in heart for they shall see God.

Matthew 5:8

Rutabagas and Fitting In

I'VE SPENT A LOT OF MY LIFE NOT KNOWING WHERE I FIT IN. I've never had one particular talent or trait that made me stand out. In elementary school, this led to feeling awkward and lonely a lot of the time. Teachers could always count on a wise crack from me because at least if someone was laughing, I felt like they were noticing me. In middle and high school, I never belonged to any particular group. I could be friends with anyone, and wandered between the jocks and cheerleaders, the party crowd, the nerds, and preppies. Even in my adult life I have found it difficult to figure out exactly where I belong.

One such instance occurred a couple of years ago. Having homeschooled my three daughters, we became part of a creative writing co-op, which included other local home school families. While the kids worked on creative writing assignments or dramas, the moms would gather in another room to have tea and chat. It was a great group of ladies who were all cordial and kind. But each month, when we gathered, I didn't feel like I fit in. My mind would race. *Maybe my make-up was a bit too heavy? My clothes a little too form fitting? I was probably a little too loud for their liking. My jokes were always met with blank stares.*

My good friend would laugh nervously along with me and try to make things not so awkward. I would leave each week convinced that they stayed behind me to pray for me as I'm sure they believed I was really a heathen needing salvation.

One day, while our girls were working in the other room, I found myself with one of the other moms having a very detailed conversation about rutabagas. I have nothing against rutabagas. I use them in fall recipes, and they can be quite yummy. But there I was acting like they were a passion of mine. We discussed the different varieties, how well they grow in the Virginia soil, and when to harvest them. My friend kept looking at me with her big blue eyes as I offered up my two cents on this fascinating root vegetable. She knew I was full of it.

Honest to Pete, what was I doing? Trying to fit in, that's what! And it wasn't working. I think this lady knew I wasn't really interested, and my friend knew I knew nothing about gardening. I knew I was not being authentic, so the whole ordeal felt miserable. I eventually stopped meeting with this group and feeling yet again that I didn't fit in. (If you are a teenager reading this, understand that your adult parents still feel like you do sometimes.)

> *Each one of us has a different skill set and personality, all to draw people to Jesus and accomplish different things for the kingdom.*

I was telling the rutabaga story to someone the other day and she pointed out something so sweet to me. God made us all different and the Body of Christ is made up of so many unique people and parts that there is no reason for us to feel insecure when we are being authentic. Each one of us has a different skill set and personality, all to draw people to Jesus and accomplish different things for the kingdom. 1 Corinthians 12:14-23 (NIV) says:

> *Even so the body is not made up of one part but of many.*

> *Now if the foot should say, "Because I am not a hand, I do not belong to the body," it would not for that reason stop being part of the body. And if the ear should say, "Because I am not an eye, I do not belong to the body," it would not*

for that reason stop being part of the body. If the whole body were an eye, where would the sense of hearing be? If the whole body were an ear, where would the sense of smell be? But in fact, God has placed the parts in the body, every one of them, just as he wanted them to be. If they were all one part, where would the body be? As it is, there are many parts, but one body.

The eye cannot say to the hand, "I don't need you!" And the head cannot say to the feet, "I don't need you!" On the contrary, those parts of the body that seem to be weaker are indispensable, and the parts that we think are less honorable we treat with special honor.

We all need one another. The folks who seem so very different from us, are very different for good reason. Everyone has a function! Some people are feet, and some are eyes. Some folks are meant to cultivate rutabagas, and some are meant to tell funny stories. Each person's gifting should be celebrated and honored not compared or judged. When we compare ourselves to others in order to determine our worth, we have taken our eyes off of the One who gets the real say over that. In turn, we have also hurt the Body that we are meant to care for and build up with our unique abilities. Nothing productive happens when we do this. But the enemy sure enjoys it when we waste our precious time and talent, or when we present an inauthentic witness.

I'm finding myself more comfortable with me these days and in less awkward situations. I am still not totally sure of my purpose here but I believe God reveals a little more of that each day. I am now able to recognize that much of my insecurity is because I am used to comparing and not honoring and I need to learn some new habits. I can just listen and learn about rutabagas and not have to pretend to be a root vegetable farmer. And I should probably assume better of the ladies around me as well, who were likely not holding prayer meetings behind my back. My insecurities impacted my perception of the entire environment around me!

Address the Mess:

The next time you have a rutabaga moment remember just one line of today's Bible selection:

> *But in fact, God has placed the parts in the body, every one*
> *of them, just as he wanted them to be.*

1 Corinthians 12:18 (NIV)

Next, take an honest inventory of the gifts and talents God has given you. How do you use them to further God's kingdom? Are you holding something back from Him or others because you don't feel good enough? Or because you don't think you will fit in? Ask Him to provide one opportunity this week to contribute to the Body of Christ in your very own unique way. And then take Him up on that opportunity.

Sermon Notes

Old Dog, New Tricks

SOMETIMES WE THINK WE ALREADY KNOW IT ALL. Just take a look at any heated debate on Facebook and you will likely find many reflections of that. We tend to be comfortable in the knowledge we have, as though in certain subjects, we have completed our learning. We are like old dogs without interest in learning new tricks. Honestly, who are we to think there is nothing more to learn, in any subject? When we don't want to open our minds to learning new things, or when we witness someone else refuse newness and change, we often use the phrase, "you can't teach an old dog new tricks." I think Jesus knows differently.

In John Chapter 3, we learn the story of Nicodemus. Nicodemus was a Pharisee—the most religious, educated, rule-following type of Jew. This man would have known the law and scriptures back and forth. He would have been held to a standard of keeping every commandment, attending every church service and completing every scheduled sacrifice. By the rigorous standards he was held to, this man should have had it all figured out. Yet he sought out the Savior late one night, under the cover of darkness.

Nicodemus clearly needed something more than rules, religion, and rigidity. When Jesus tells Nicodemus that someone must be born again in order to experience the fullness of God's kingdom, Nicodemus produces an "old dog, new tricks" response:

*How can someone be born again when he is old? Can he
enter into his mother's womb a second time and be born?*

John 3:4 (NKJV)

I imagine Jesus staring into the fire with a slight smile, shaking His holy
head a little. This older, wiser gentleman named Nicodemus just didn't get
it. Thankfully our Lord is patient, and tenderhearted.

Our rebirth is not a physical rebirth but a reorientation. It's a change of
heart which recognizes that a world based on ourselves, and our feelings,
and preferences, over the commands of God, is not the Kingdom of God,
but the kingdom of ME. In order to enjoy all that God has to offer, which
includes eternal life, we must admit our need for Him and be reborn as His
creation, not the creation of our earthly parents. We must be reoriented
to a world revolving around Him, and not us, or our earthly standards, or
earthly heritage.

Jesus continues to explain. And tucked away in this late-night conversation
is the most famous verse ever written, John 3:16:

*For God so loved the world that he gave his only son that
whoever believes in him shall not perish but have eternal
life.*

How about that? This verse was spoken first to the most religious, knowl-
edgeable man of the time. Jesus did not choose the leper, the prostitute,
or the thief, to share with this amazing truth—He chose the old dog. He
chose the one who would likely not realize his need for a reorientation.

Jesus informs Nicodemus that He did not come to condemn the world but
to save. Perhaps Jesus knew that Nicodemus felt condemned by his standards of religiosity. The world of the Pharisee was one of guilt and shame
covered by routine and ritual. Despite the religious orientation of his life,
I believe Nicodemus loved God, but the question is, did Nicodemus know
that God so loved him?

Often in our Christian walk, we focus our attention on all that we see going wrong in the world. Immoral choices, blatant sin, and depravity receive much of our attention, prayers, and criticism. The conversation of John 3 tells me that God is just as concerned with the thoughts and hearts of those who don't think they need Him; the ones who think they are cleaned up and good enough; the ones who know their Bibles cover to cover, and can sing hymns by heart.

> *Despite the religious orientation of his life, I believe Nicodemus loved God, but the question is, did Nicodemus know that God so loved him?*

I find myself in the "old dog" camp often and it has not served me well. When I think I've heard it all before, and know it all, I miss the grace and love of Jesus and begin to absorb the guilt and condemnation of my own thoughts and this world. I pray to be like Nicodemus, who despite his "position" and "knowledge," sought the Savior because he knew He had so much more to offer than a religion of our own making.

Address the Mess:

Use this moment to consider the religious rituals you partake in. Is your heart truly in them? Be completely honest with yourself. Are you doing them because you think you should, or because you genuinely want to? None of us are perfectly holy in our desires. Take a look at the ways that you participate in religious ritual and examine if that ritual still should have a place in your life, or if you need a reorientation to participate in it, with the right heart.

Sermon Notes

Little Foxes

I N MY PART OF THE WORLD, FOXES ARE A CELEBRATED CREATURE. The age-old sport of fox hunting is still practiced. One can find many household items portraying their image such as embroidered pillows, corkscrews, tableware, you name it. The fox is known for being beautiful, quick, crafty, and cunning.

Yet there is a little verse tucked inside the sultry love story of Song of Solomon that references these animals in a more cautionary way. Verse 2:15 says, "Catch the foxes for us, the little foxes that spoil the vineyards, for our vineyards are in blossom." Pastors and Bible teachers will often remind us to be careful of the little foxes that ruin the vineyard. The precaution is wise. This small creature, not much bigger than a large rodent, can decimate a crop or entire hen house. He is known to pick off his enemy one by one, and go unnoticed, often creeping around at night.

What are the little foxes in our lives? During the time of Lent, we are called to give up something to enter into a more intimate time with the Lord as we prepare to celebrate His death and resurrection. Many people choose to give up sweets or rich foods, others go on a social media fast and deactivate their Facebook account for a period. Whatever is a distraction from their relationship with the Lord is set aside for a time.

I believe God honors our times of fasting. We are called to fast and pray many times throughout the Bible. Many prayer warriors credit fasting with revelation and renewal and answer to prayer. But what about the little foxes? What are the little things that creep into our lives and pick at our marriages, our relationships with children and other family members? Who are the little foxes that spoil our time with the Lord throughout the year and interfere with our communion with the Holy Spirit?

Little foxes usually aren't obvious until you see the damage they've done. They can hide tucked away in friendships, hobbies and even religious activity. I once heard a story about a mother who loved the Lord so much, she spent all her time in church and her family never saw her. Satan loves it when our religious activity erodes our family time. Perhaps it's a friendship that is so consistently negative that we walk away from every conversation feeling torn down and negative about ourselves. Maybe it's our music, movie or television selection; the supposed "harmless" entertainment that picks away at our conscience so that we become desensitized to sex or violence.

> *I once heard a story about a mother who loved the Lord so much, she spent all her time in church and her family never saw her. Satan loves it when our religious activity erodes our family time.*

During a time of reflection, (whether it be Lent or not), we might consider the little foxes and be vigilant to ask the Lord to help us catch them. We need Him to help us catch them *and remove them* before they take down the vineyards that we've been so careful to build. How many marriages that were lovingly cultivated might be saved if both husband and wife reflected on the little foxes that are currently tearing them apart? How many families might have an easier time at the dinner table if words were spoken a little more gently and thoughtfully? Which addictions might be conquered if we took notice of the little things that drive us towards them? What might thrive and blossom, if finally freed from the marauders?

Address the Mess:

Get honest. The little foxes of deception and denial cause dramatic damage when left to run wild. And getting honest with yourself may be one of the most difficult tasks to do. Let's do it together.

You already know how and where you spend time, money and energy, that does not glorify the Lord. You don't even have to come up with a brilliant plan like a farmer who seeks to outwit the fox. You can put a stop or end to your little foxes quite easily. End the relationship, stop watching or reading the trash, get rid of the social media account, stop the compulsive ministry effort that is removing you from your family, block the text, the channel or the interaction. Remember your family is like a flock of tender little chicks. The foxes in your life will easily take them out if you don't take care of them. Catch and acknowledge a fox today and deal with him appropriately.

Remember I said let's do it together? This isn't any easier for me just because I've typed the words. We've got to set out the traps.

Pray with me...

Lord, we rely on you. We ask you to guard our hearts; your vineyard within us. Cultivate in us, a love and devotion towards You and the people You love. Find the little foxes, Lord. Show us who and what they are, and remove them once and for all. What seems like great effort for us, is no effort at all, for You. Thank you for Your strength, Almighty Father. In Jesus's name, we pray, Amen.

Sermon Notes

Sweet Sixteen

I WAS AWAY FROM MY HUSBAND ON A MISSION TRIP for our sixteenth anniversary. It was hard to be away, and my teammates were so kind to surprise me with what I am sure was the only bowl of mint chocolate chip ice cream in La Croix, Haiti. I had to eat it quickly as it was melting in the ninety-degree heat.

As I thought about our anniversary, I realized that if our marriage was a person, we would be having a "sweet sixteen" party and the "person" would be excited to be able to get its driver's license. It's fun to put time into that sort of perspective. But our sixteen-year marriage doesn't quite feel like an inexperienced sixteen-year-old. It feels a little bit wiser, although a text or phone call from my man still gives me butterflies as though we were teenagers; and I still love to flirt with him.

Even though we are still relatively young and our kids are young, we've been through a lot. The only way you build muscle is with a workout and our marriage muscles have been tested. One of our favorite verses comes from one of King David's prayers of gratitude. 2 Samuel 7:18 says,

> *Who am I, O Lord God, and what is my house that you have brought me thus far?*

David spoke this prayer after many years of hardships. Not only had David been chosen as an unlikely king of Israel, he had conquered giant, ferocious enemies and was chased by a madman for years, narrowly surviving. My husband and I look at the past sixteen years with gratitude and say, "Who are we, that we would be brought so far?" So many relational attacks and grenades were launched into our marriage early on, by the ten-year mark, we should have imploded and surrendered.

But the love and forgiveness of Christ and the exceptional support from family and friends triumphed. In the midst of the most difficult days, my mother reminded me to "give thanks in all things," as the Scripture says in 1 Thessalonians 5:18. She reminded me that the Lord's desire was for my husband to be whole and well and for me to allow God to work through me. We learned that with Christ, all things really are possible (Matthew 19:26). These verses aren't just nice platitudes embroidered on your grandma's throw pillows; they are eternal truths.

The thing about David's prayer of gratitude, is that it falls smack in the middle of the account of his life. Yes, he had defeated Goliath and the Philistines. Yes, he had outrun crazy Saul who sought to destroy him. But he had not yet encountered Bathsheba. He had not yet committed adultery or set up the murder of his mistress's husband. His son had not yet committed rape and incest. Some might say the future held far worse things. I think it's important to note this. I love my husband and know we are both new people because of the cleansing of Christ, but life will still offer its difficulties—Jesus promised us that. It's important for us to stand on God's promises, to give thanks for where we have come, but also be wise and watchful so that we are not ensnared by the enemy who would seek to kill and destroy the covenant of marriage.

So, I think it's ok for me to celebrate my marriage like a giddy teenager focuses on her crush. I thank God for where we are today, and I ask Him to protect us from future troubles. I will seek the wisdom of those who have gone before us in this marriage walk successfully. Most importantly, we will rely on Christ's love to be the bond between us.

Address the Mess:

I'm going to make this one really simple. If you are married, flirt with your husband today. I don't care where you are at, I want you to do something purposely sweet (and maybe even a little sexy) to remind him of who you once were when you fell in love with him. If things are tough and you can't bring yourself to be directly vulnerable, maybe send him a song that can remind you both of better times together. (Of course, if you're a man reading this, follow the same instruction toward your wife.)

If you are single, I want you to do something that may be equally challenging. I want you to thank God for the season you are in and the protection He's provided you from relationships that weren't meant to be bonded in holy matrimony. I want you to thank Him for the areas that He's healed from those relationships. Additionally, I want you to go and do something that you uniquely enjoy. I'm not suggesting you empty the bank account to go on a lavish shopping spree, I'm talking about a simple pleasure. Go get your favorite ice cream and sit in your favorite spot to enjoy it. Watch your favorite movie. Cook a fancy meal for yourself and don't forget dessert. Take the time to read a book for pleasure. Do something that you can enjoy freely in this season of singleness without distraction, and then thank God for being right there with you in the provisions.

Sermon Notes

_____
_____
_____
_____
_____
_____
_____
_____
_____
_____
_____
_____
_____
_____
_____
_____
_____
_____
_____
_____
_____
_____
_____
_____

Mission ... Impossible to Ignore

I HAVE HOMESCHOOLED MY CHILDREN FOR OVER TEN YEARS and the area where I live is filled with many home school families. However, I still draw attention from adults with inquisitive looks when I am out during the day with my children. When we are in places where there aren't any other homeschoolers, folks will automatically say, "Aren't they supposed to be in school?" We smile and say that we home school and most folks say something like, "Oh, that's cool." Some ask questions of my girls such as, "What's that like?" or "Do you like it?" We have even experienced others who go further to say, "When are you going to *let* them go to school?"

I try to assume the last question is well-meaning but I can't help that it conjures up a picture in my head of my children being tied to chairs in a dark basement held against their will. And while it's really no one's business, I then explain that we enjoy our lifestyle and how the kids have a say in how they are schooled. Some then ask, "What happened," as if the only reason to homeschool is some horrible bullying situation or learning disability. While events certainly contributed and led up to our decision, I realize now that home schooling is my mission field. It's a mission I felt strongly that I could not ignore.

Prior to homeschooling, my husband and I could see our children and many other children feeling lost and swallowed up in their schools. We could see that they were not learning to love others or to love learning. I don't blame the schools entirely for this, I believe many factors were at play.

175

The world at large is faster paced, and childhood has been drastically short-ened. My husband and I felt as though there was a tidal wave approach-ing our home and as we prayed for direction, the answer we consistently received was, "Bring them home."

We don't judge those who choose to send their children to public or private school. There is an answer for everyone. But we have a choice in how we raise our children and we don't have to follow the crowds. As parents, we must choose what fits our family structure the best. We must choose what is best for our kids. Not because the alternatives are inherently bad, but because kids and families have individual needs. Home schooling is my mission field right now. I feel strongly that I can pour into my daughters right here, in a way I might not be able to otherwise.

God sets inside each person a purpose and a mission. It takes a lot of prayer and listening and watching to understand what that is. Sometimes that purpose is only for a season, sometimes it's for life. I can't imagine that anyone ever approached Mother Teresa and said, "So, when are you going to give this up and get a husband and a secretarial position somewhere?" That would be absurd. You don't interrupt a mission. When God gives you a vision for your purpose, you obey and follow through because you are doing His work.

Consider Nehemiah. Nehemiah was purposed to build a wall to protect his community. In Nehemiah Chapter 6, messengers were sent several times to distract him from his work and asked him to come down off his wall to speak with them. Nehemiah replied, "I am doing a great work and I cannot come down. Why should the work stop while I leave it and come down to you?" So, when the well-meaning friend asks, "When are you going to let them go to school?" I may reply, "We are doing great work here and we cannot come down."

Missions aren't always easy, and sometimes they look messy. I'm sure Nehemiah hammered his own thumb a time or two. Sometimes my mis-sion is messy, and I get tired. Sometimes I'd like to come off my wall and run to Starbucks with a friend and drown myself in a Chai Latte. There's something peaceful about being where God wants you to be, even when it's different from what everyone else is doing.

Some people rescue animals, others feed the hungry, and some teach reading to the illiterate. When God calls you to something, you shouldn't stop yourself from doing it. You know immediately, deep down that this is your purpose. He does this on purpose, making it impossible to ignore.

> ***There's something peaceful about being where God wants you to be, even when it's different from what everyone else is doing.***

Address the Mess:

What is the mission God has placed on your heart? It doesn't have to be across the world, it could be like mine; it could be something right in your very home. Now, what would it take to start? Be specific in your answer. Do one thing this week to start—research, make a phone call, schedule time to start. Don't waste any more time not doing what God has called you to. Now take it one step further into the uncomfortable reality of this becoming your reality. Tell a friend what you are doing and ask to be held accountable. Really. Do it.

Sermon Notes

On the Altar

When they came to the place of which God had told him,
Abraham built the altar there and laid the wood in order
and bound Isaac his son and laid him on the altar, on top of
the wood.

Genesis 22:9

I T HAD BEEN A YEAR OF CELEBRATION AND EXCITEMENT FOR MY FAMI- LY. My oldest graduated high school, my middle child found purpose and success in new endeavors after challenging health issues, and my youngest child finished elementary school. We didn't arrive at the celebrations without going through some heartaches though.

My older children decided about a year ago to leave a sport that had been near and dear to their hearts. They knew the time, money, and effort that horseback riding required would not align with new interests, goals, and the realities of the future. As my middle daughter and I drove away from their barn with their beautiful homemade tack trunk in the back of my truck we listened to a song on the radio with lyrics that hit home in the moment. The song spoke of fresh starts as the result of something dear ending. My daughter looked out the window and cried quietly and I pretended not to notice or cry too hard, myself.

I recently shared with a new friend the challenges of raising children and sending them off into the world and how contrary that feels to my spirit.

God gave me my three beautiful daughters to protect and guard, (and I do so fiercely), and now I'm supposed to let them go? Is this some kind of joke? My mother had warned me about the conflicting feelings of motherhood for years and I chalked it up to cliché advice, but as always, my mother was right.

Thinking on this brought me to the story of Abraham and Isaac. Abraham and Sarah waited a lifetime for a child of their own. They went through enormous turmoil waiting on their bodies to produce their very own offspring. They made terrible mistakes along the way, repented and returned to God many times, but were finally rewarded with their very own son. They named him "Isaac," which means "laughter" because Sarah couldn't believe this dream was finally coming true. And then in Genesis 22, God presents an unthinkable command. He calls to Abraham to take his one and only son to the land of Moriah and sacrifice Isaac on an altar. I can only imagine Abraham thinking, "You mean to tell me this child I prayed for, waited for, delighted in, doted on, is now just another sacrifice?"

We know that faithful Abraham took Isaac up that dreadful hill, bound him, and that God ultimately provided a ram in the thicket as a substitute for Isaac, (which foreshadowed Christ as our substitute). Whew! But how and why was Abraham able to go through with it? Isn't that the kind of obedience, strength, and spiritual fortitude we all want?

Perhaps it's because Abraham put himself on that altar first. No, not physically, but spiritually. From the time Abraham first heard from God that he was to leave his home and go to where God showed him, Abraham sacrificed what he thought his life would look like. God made a covenant with Abraham through Abraham's obedience to sacrifice and divide several creatures and Abraham

> **Abraham knew very early on that by putting his own life on God's altar that God would be near and walk among the broken and bloodied parts.**

watched God pass between the pieces of sacrifice. Abraham knew very early on that by putting his own life on God's altar that God would be near and walk among the broken and bloodied parts. This covenant would be for all of Abraham's offspring—but only because Abraham did exactly what God told him to do and essentially give up the right to life as he thought it should be.

> *The only reason he was able to get that far is because he knew his God was faithful and because he already put his own wants and desires on God's altar.*

That's exactly what parents do. Parents give up much of their own rights in order to make a way for their children. Mothers start by sharing their bodies and giving their life over to create a beautiful new human being. Moms and dads sacrifice many nights of sleep to rock, feed, and sing to their babies. As kids get older, we spend hours in the car on the way to doctors' appointments, recitals, tutors, and sporting events. And after all of that, we launch them. It hurts and it's scary and it doesn't feel right. Abraham probably thought all of these things as he bound Isaac and raised the knife. The only reason he was able to get that far is because he knew his God was faithful and because he already put his own wants and desires on God's altar.

Address the Mess:

Whether you are a parent or not, when have you needed to put your own needs on the altar to realize that God had something better? Perhaps you delayed a purchase you wanted, or gave up a relationship that you wanted, but realized wasn't good for you. Perhaps you were a caregiver to a child or a relative. Sometimes the more we invest, the more unlikely we are to want to hand it back to God. What area of your life would have you have the hardest time today, placing on the altar if God asked you to? Is there an issue of unbelief in your heart related to that?

Sermon Notes

Shine On

*After six days Jesus took with him Peter, James and John
the brother of James, and led them up a high mountain by
themselves. There he was transfigured before them. His face
shone like the sun, and his clothes became as white as the
light.*

Matthew 17:1-2

ONE DAY, I WAS AT THE COUNTER OF A LOCAL COFFEE SHOP with a friend, and we were deciding what to order for lunch. As we pondered the menu, the gal waiting on us complimented my friend and said, "Oh my gosh, you have the most beautiful skin! Your face just shines, what in the world do you do?"

My friend was smiling, and I could tell the compliment took her by surprise. I looked at her and it was true, she was simply glowing. She thanked the young girl and tried to think of what exactly in her skincare routine was responsible for such great results and I quickly jumped in and said, "Oh, that's the Lord! She spends a lot of time with Him, doesn't it look good on her?"

We laughed and the girl at the counter who was also a Christian said, "Wow, I need to do more of that!" It's true about my friend. This gal is walking hand in hand with Jesus right now through some exciting and terrifying times. She prays constantly, worships fervently, and serves selflessly.

183

The beauty on her face doesn't come from a jar, she's been transfigured.

The gospels give accounts of Jesus's own transfiguration. I once heard transfiguration described as a complete change of form or appearance into a more beautiful or spiritual state. It's hard to believe that the Son of God, Himself, could even become more beautiful or more spiritual. Yet God wanted us to see that Jesus in His human form had the ability to achieve more spiritual beauty. Jesus took his best buddies to the top of a mountain to get a break from the madness and monotony, (which can even be found in our own ministry efforts). I think He needed a minute. And there in the quietness, God was able to bathe Jesus in His glory.

Moses had a similar experience after spending time with the Lord. He also went up to commune with God and seek Him because the weight and responsibility of leadership was too much. Exodus 34:29 (NIV) says:

> *When Moses came down from Mount Sinai with the two tablets of the covenant law in his hands, he was not aware that his face was radiant because he had spoken with the Lord.*

Like my friend, Moses was not even aware of his radiance. And notice that no major effort was made by either Jesus or Moses to transform their appearance. They simply spent time with the Lord and allowed Him to do the work.

On one mission trip to Haiti, our team had the task of building a huge playground for the children who live in extreme poverty. This playground is located next the constantly burning trash pile for the mission nearby, but the surrounding mountain ranges and smiles of beautiful children make the burning trash hardly noticeable. We worked together in the heat for days to erect this symbol of childhood innocence in a land stricken with extreme poverty. We sang praise music, prayed together at mealtimes and at night, we shared testimonies of how God worked in our lives. By the end of the trip, our faces also shined like sun.

Address the Mess:

You don't have to go to another country, or even to the top of a hill, to spend time with God. The Bible says He waits for us to come to Him. Challenge yourself to set aside a special time and place to meet with Him. Guard your schedule and space from distraction. "Take a minute" like Jesus did, to just go bask with His Father. Think of all the ways He loves you and make room for a heart-to-heart conversation with Him, just you two. Take note of how it changes you.

Sermon Notes

Store Bought Cookies

CHRISTMASTIME BRINGS PARTIES, lunches, gift exchanges, parades, and other kinds of events. For moms, especially, the weight of the season can be too much. All the lists to complete, rooms to clean, presents to wrap, cards to sign, and cookies to bake. But what about when life is too much and you can't make your family's Christmas match the Christmas board on your Pinterest account?

I was listening to Christmas carols in the car one day feeling like they also tend to taunt us this time of year if we have a struggle of some sort. I used to love the song, "Have Yourself a Merry Little Christmas" as a kid, but as an adult now I don't always find my heart feeling "light" as the song commands me to do. I started talking back to the radio one day saying, "My yuletide is not gay and my troubles are nowhere near from far away!" In fact, it seems troubles are closer at hand every year.

Even in times where illness and tragedy seem to run rampant in the world, the ugly sweater invites and requests for treats and wrapped gifts still arrive. Here's the thing, sometimes you have to give yourself permission to bring the store-bought cookies to the very fancy table. It's ok to take the easy way out during a tough time. I don't recommend withdrawing from the world completely; there is hope and healing in fellowship. But we don't have to outdo Martha Stewart just to be there. Our true friends will understand.

I'm making my way to a few gatherings in the season. Some tables will surely have over-the-top crafts and homemade treats. My offering will likely be a box of store-bought cookies which I will choose hastily and purchase in the self-checkout that doesn't work properly. My kids will be waiting in the car while it's running and I probably won't even put those cookies on my own plate, I'll pull them from the ugly grocery bag and pop open the plastic clam shell container on the table next to the cheese sticks made to look like snowmen with cute faces and little scarves.

It's ok. We're all in different places each year. Some are celebrating, some are meh, and some are sad. No matter where we are, we must give ourselves grace. God didn't send His Son to run us ragged. He sent Him to take our burdens and to show us unconditional love. God sent Him to turn what the world expects upside down and do the unexpected. God gave us Jesus so that the government would be upon His shoulders not ours. Jesus is our Prince of Peace not the Prince of Pinterest. Jesus came and redeemed us whether we pipe the royal icing or run through the self-checkout. Keep your mind and heart fixed on Him, and not the world's expectations at Christmas.

Address the Mess:

What's an area of your life where you need to give yourself permission to "phone it in?" Maybe you need to quit an activity, relinquish a leadership position, or simply buy some store-bought cookies instead of making some from scratch. Identify one area of your life causing you constant angst and do one thing to change it. You don't owe anyone explanations.

Sermon Notes

He Wasn't Born for That

ONE YEAR, AROUND THE HOLIDAYS, I was pondering how the annual gatherings would take place and all the things that go along with coordinating them. Who would host, who would visit, what foods would be prepared, and which gifts needed to be sent where? I could already see how certain things were overlapping. The stomachache began as I realized I couldn't be in three places at once, and not everyone was going to be happy. If you're a man reading this, you're likely saying, "They'll get over it" and you're rolling your eyes, but seriously, most women just want everyone to be happy.

As I paced around my kitchen working out the logistics in my mind, I heard that still small voice whisper, "He wasn't born for that." No matter how much I tried to push it away, again and again, "He wasn't born for that." Well I know that! I've done the Bible studies; I never miss a Sunday of advent and I sing in the choir! No need to tell me.

Except, I needed to hear it that day, and every day. Every day that I feel the guilt that I have had to decline an invitation or have forgotten to make some treat. On the days where the children continue to add to their Christmas lists, even though we told them to choose three items. When I see the beautiful decorations in a friend's home and wonder if I have let my family down because mine is more modestly adorned. He wasn't born for that.

So, I began to really ponder what Jesus came to this earth to accomplish.

We love to say, "Jesus is the 'Reason for the Season," but what does that really mean? Here is a list that trumps any Christmas cooking and to-do list:

1.Jesus came so that we might have a full, abundant life (John 10:10).

2. He was born to be the Son of mankind, our Wonderful Counselor and our Everlasting Father (Isaiah 9:6).

3. He came to bring peace (Isaiah 9:6).

4. Jesus was born to do more than we could possibly ask or imagine (Ephesians 3:20).

5. The Son of God was born so that all fear and oppression would cease and the ground would be leveled once and for all at the cross (Isaiah 54).

6. Christ came for freedom and for freedom He has set us free (Gal 5:1).

7. He came to shepherd us and lay down His life for us (John 10:14-15).

8. He came to be love in a person (1 John 4:8).

9. He came to destroy what was known of religion and offer mankind a relationship with the living God (Matthew 23).

10. He came to die (Hebrews 2:9).

This list has become my focus as I count down the days until Christmas. Jesus came not for cookie recipes and credit card bills. He came for so much more and for us to live out this truth each day. Families need to know this. Women need to know this. The world is hungry to know all of this, now more than ever.

While some would have us believe that Jesus is mocked and irrelevant, I would bet my last dollar that His love is desperately desired, and when given genuinely, and generously, is irresistible. So, when the stacks of catalogs arrive each day or the requests for my time and money pile up, I will simply repeat, "He wasn't born for that" and look for where His love is needed most, at that moment.

Address the Mess:

What are some religious activities or rituals you take part in, that you only do to check a box? There's nothing wrong with reverence and rituals if they truly draw us closer to the Lord, but if we are honest, there are some things we do, just to please ourselves or man. Think about it—when our spouse only goes through the motions with us, do we feel loved? Identify the "going through the motion" moments in your relationship with the Lord, and make some changes. He wasn't born for ritual with you. He was born for relationship.

Sermon Notes

_____

_____

_____

_____

_____

_____

_____

_____

_____

_____

_____

_____

_____

_____

_____

_____

_____

_____

_____

_____

_____

_____

_____

_____

_____

_____

Section 7

Blessed are the peacemakers for they shall be called sons of God.

Matthew 5:9

On the Mission Field, at Macy's

MY DAUGHTERS WERE ASKED TO BE JUNIOR BRIDESMAIDS in my cousin's wedding. So, one Friday, my mom, my three girls, and myself made the trip to a large shopping mall to find dresses for the occasion. The bride was considerate to allow the girls to choose their own dress as long as it was a coordinating color. While that task seemed simple enough, with three girls and three very different styles and opinions, I knew we'd have challenges before us.

My oldest had instant success and I breathed a sigh of relief. I thought surely this was a sign from God that we would be in and out in a flash, but no. For the next hour, we began to wander from store to store and into every boutique with a dress in the window. We had trouble finding anything suitable for the other two. (Can I just say there are not many appropriate dresses for preteen girls?) I knew we still had miles to go when my youngest daughter found something but announced that it was extremely itchy, not comfortable, and concluded that she might not be able to hold her flowers still because of it. *Sigh.*

Thirst and hunger began to set in, but we pushed onward. My 12-year-old was extremely forlorn and believed she would *never* find anything. I reminded her that this wedding was not about her and that surely a dress existed that would suffice. Tension mounting between us, everything I said was received with a sigh and an eye roll. When we spotted Macy's just ahead, I suggested we go in and give it a try. As we wearily walked toward the back of the store, we saw color, sequins, silk and taffeta. We became hopeful that we were in the midst of the solution.

My daughter found several possible dresses and we headed to the dressing room. Outside of the fitting rooms, there was a sitting area, and a man in his late 50s or 60s sat there on a bench, reading his phone. (May I say that husbands who sit outside dressing rooms and hold purses are a special sort?) Knowing how exasperated my 12-year-old was, and how tired we all were, I looked at my mom and other daughters who plopped down with their packages on another bench, and I folded my hands and began praying out loud. "Dear Jesus, we need one of these dresses to work, please encourage us with the right dress. Amen." I opened my eyes and asked my mom, "You think Jesus cares about this?" She said, "I'm sure Jesus cares, yes." I raised my hand to the ceiling and said, "Thank you, Jesus."

The sweet man by the door looked at me and said, "Jesus? You know Jesus?" I looked at him and sat down by him and said, "Oh yes!" In the back of my mind, I wondered if I had offended him. My mom told him that Jesus was our friend. He then told us that he knew Jesus as a prophet and a teacher. I countered and said, "He was much more than that, Jesus is God!" My mom and daughter became quiet and turned to face him. He smiled and I smiled, and he replied, "Jesus never called himself God in the Bible. Do all of you Christians really believe that?"

"Oh, yes", I said, "Jesus says He is the Way, the Truth and the Life, and no one comes to the Father but through Him. Jesus calls Himself the door. If you want to know the Father, you must walk through the door and that means you accept Jesus and believe in salvation through Jesus. He is equal to the Father." I encouraged him to read the Book of John. He nodded and was genuinely interested and maybe even a little intrigued. I then asked him if he had heard of the Trinity - the Father, Son and Holy Spirit. I said each person is separate and one at the same time. He shook his head as if this was unbelievable. I said, "How about water? You know water, right?" He nodded. I continued telling him that water can be liquid, solid and gas, but it's still water. I explained that God is like this. He is the Father, He is the Son, and He is the Holy Spirit.

At this point, the fitting room area felt like there was a palpable electricity in the air. I asked where he was from and he said Dubai. He described life there and how he came to the United States to get his daughter a bone marrow transplant. We listened as he explained about her condition and we encouraged him regarding her treatment. He and his wife were attending an upcoming wedding as well, and he was waiting on his wife who was also seeking the right dress.

My daughter then appeared wearing one of her choices and the man saw her first. He grinned and said, "She is beautiful! Is she yours?" As she came into my view, it looked as though a fairy godmother had fit her with the perfect dress! She was lovely and demure. She was so pleased with herself and I breathed a prayer of thanksgiving and a sigh of relief.

It was getting late into the evening and we had a long drive home. I stood up and thanked the man for our discussion and explained we needed to purchase our dress and go home. (I was secretly afraid my daughter would change her mind and would want to search longer! We had to seal the deal!) We made our way to the cashier and he thanked us for our chat, and we all smiled and nodded.

I was stunned. Stunned that God would use a girls' shopping trip for bridesmaid dresses, to share the love of His son. I had originally told my daughter that the dress was not about her, it was about the bride. But in reality, it was about the Bride of Christ. It was God using us to open wide the gates of Heaven for one of His precious children. I realized we were led to that department store at that perfect moment to encounter this man and to share about the perfect love of the Father and His Son, Jesus. Even though this man was of a different religion and culture, he was open to hearing, and we were open towards sharing with him. There was no heated debate, only an exchange. No one wished harm or ill, we each sought understanding.

With this occurrence, 1 Peter 3:15 became real to me for the first time:

> *But in your hearts honor Christ the Lord as holy, always*
> *being prepared to make a defense to anyone who asks you for*
> *a reason for the hope that is in you; yet do it with gentleness*
> *and respect...*

One never knows where they might encounter someone seeking to know Christ. In my case, it was not where I was expecting, especially in my weary state. It may not always be the places you expect, either. God can use you anywhere, even at the shopping mall. Are you prepared?

I forgot to get this man's name so I could pray for him by name, but God knows who He is. I pray he is one step closer to knowing that Jesus was more than just a good man, a prophet and a teacher. I pray my daughters were encouraged that God uses all things for His glory, including long trips to the shopping mall.

Address the Mess:

The next time you're out, pray to God to show you someone with whom you can share your faith. If you're new and nervous about this, don't worry, it's really not so scary! You might start by looking the cashier in the eye at the grocery store and tell them you thank God for them, or you will be praying for them this week. Perhaps you pray out loud with someone in the waiting room at the doctor's office. Look for your divine appointment in the mundane errands of the week. You may be surprised at the reaction you receive. We often wrongly assume people don't want us to bless them or pray for them. Yet no one has ever rebuked me for being kind and sharing the love of Christ. Change your outlook to consider each time you leave your home as a mission trip! You'll look at your errands in a much different way, and likely with much greater purpose.

Sermon Notes

Unwilling to Shame

G ROUP BIBLE STUDY HAS BEEN ONE OF THE MOST HEALING ACTIVI-
TIES in my life. Often, I will find myself trudging through tough
things and God combines His word and His people to bring fresh
water to dry places in my life.

In one particular study of Matthew, I initially approached it with a sense
of pride. Having grown up in church, it appeared there was nothing much
new for me to learn, and I skimmed over some verses and questions thinking I had heard it all before. And that's where God stepped in and showed
me that His Word is indeed still living and active and sharper than a dou-
bled edged sword (Heb 4:12). He showed me one of the beloved characters
of Jesus's birth in a completely new way.

The scripture tells us of how Joseph learns of Mary's pregnancy. Given the
circumstances, this could have been dire, as these two had not yet consum-
mated their relationship. I can only imagine the shame, anger, and embarrassment Joseph must have felt as Mary explained her unbelievable situation
with a quivering voice. For the first time in reading this story, I realized that
before the revelation and explanation from God's angel, Joseph was unwilling to put his betrothed wife to shame. Verse 1:19 says:

> *And her husband Joseph, being a just man and unwilling to*
> *put her to shame, resolved to divorce her quietly.*

The punishment for adultery at this time was stoning and death. And before ending the life of the guilty party, the offender was publicly tormented and tortured. Joseph had every reason to begin that public display of condemnation and right the wrong done to him, but the Bible says he resolved to take care of things quietly. Joseph's actions were not just contrary to the way of doing things at his time in history, but contrary to how we handle wrongdoing in ours. Today, we take to the Internet to call out the dirty and the despicable. We may not throw stones, but we throw words. We may not kill the body, but we seek to destroy reputation.

In my own life, I have had to confess some pretty hard things to my husband. Not adultery, or murder or some other huge crime; just the little ways I've not been completely honest over the years and how they've snowballed into bigger problems. My own sins were not even malicious. In my own messed up way, I thought I was helping, when in reality, I was only creating a bigger mess.

I imagine Mary expected to be dragged out into the street upon sharing her news. I've felt like that, too. But I have learned, I married a just man who is unwilling to put me to shame. We sing about the forgiveness and redemption we receive from Jesus every week in church, but there is something so powerful when the person you hurt the most makes a decision to forgive and restore you. I have always overlooked Joseph's kindness and gentleness and sadly, I overlooked my own husband in this way, too.

Joseph continues to be a quiet hero in the story of Jesus's young life. He takes direction and warning from the Lord and guards the life of his wife and the miracle baby. Joseph set aside his own rights and desires to protect and care for the family God gave him. Surely, he was not without his moments of questioning, anger and frustration. This was likely not the life he envisioned for himself.

Some days we pray for miracles, thinking they will show themselves as immediate healing, financial windfalls, and good fortune. God is showing me that forgiveness is the greatest miracle. Especially, the forgiveness that is given from one human to another during the most painful situations. Over time, that forgiveness is what will bring about the growth and change we so desperately crave. Isn't it amazing that God used Joseph's act of forgiveness and acceptance to protect the Son of Man who would ultimately forgive and accept us all?

Address the Mess:

What if we all became unwilling to shame our spouses, our children, our friends and even our enemies, and chose to care, protect, and defend them instead? Is there someone you've recently shamed? What if you went back to them and showed them love and support instead? Showing someone love and support doesn't equal endorsement of bad behavior, it displays value and respect for the person made in the image of God, and acknowledges the source of their true worth.

Sermon Notes

The War for Independence

I**N JULY, OUR STREETS ARE ADORNED WITH THE COLORS** of red, white and blue. Parades of local marching bands, tractors pulling floats and kids on bikes with streamers slowly pass us by as we wave and shout, "Happy 4th!" We are proud of the hard-fought independence we earned as we fought British rule centuries ago. As a new country, we believed we should be autonomous and have the right to rule ourselves and not answer to a king on a throne an ocean away.

Being dependent on anyone else other than ourselves has a negative connotation. We are told to pull ourselves up by our own bootstraps. We are told that women should never depend on a man. Parents are taught to help their children to be independent from a very young age. Men are told to make their own way in the world by their own hard work. We are all told to create our own happiness and our own reality.

There is a war for independence that rages within all of us. It's not a geopolitical type of war, but one where we as individuals seek our own independence from our Creator and our Father. It began way back when Eve was offered the forbidden fruit from the serpent who asked her to question God's instruction. "Did he really say you shouldn't eat it?" (Gen 3:1). There is a wicked hint of independence rooted in this, implying that she could thrive independent of God's instructions for her life. Haven't we all heard a similar translation? *Think for yourself, girl! You don't need Him! You're missing out on so much more! Do you really believe that?*

> *Every heinous act you see on the evening news is a result of the original war for independence.*

And we all know the consequence of Adam and Eve's infamous attempt at independence—separation from God for all of us. Because of Eve and Adam's poor choice, sin entered the world, work became hard and the weeds sprang forth. Every generation that followed contended with lies, murder, pride and prejudice. Man began to live desperately for himself and not for his brother. We see it today. Kids push and pull away from the parents who were given to them for protection and care. Spouses seek to be independent from one another which results in cold or broken marriages. Every heinous act you see on your evening news is a result of the original war for independence. Sadly, we would all rather go our own way than depend on one another and ultimately God. Satan felt the same way.

Did you ever consider that Satan's attack in the Garden was targeted on Eve as to inflict the same pain on her, that he had first experienced himself? Satan was the very first one to experience the consequence of the desire to be independent. Prideful and untrusting that God's plan was best, Satan was the first to make a declaration of independence:

> *I will ascend to heaven;*
> *above the stars of God*
> *I will set my throne on high;*
> *I will sit on the mount of assembly*
> *in the far reaches of the north;*
> *I will ascend above the heights of the clouds;*
> *I will make myself like the Most High.*
>
> *Isaiah 14:13-14*

And really, why was he trying so hard to be independent? God had already blessed him with abundance. Long before the scene in the garden, the Bible says that Lucifer, (another name for Satan), was the most beautiful of God's angels. His entire being embodied worship of God. He made beautiful music and led many angels in peaceful, loving worship of the Almighty God. But one day, his own free will took over and the most beautiful guardian angel created declared his independence, forever sealing his fate.

We tend to scoff at this, refusing to identify with this account of this fallen angel, but he's not so different from us. We set ourselves on the throne of our own lives, believing we are above others or above certain situations in the world. We make ourselves kings and queens of a universe that revolves around our 1/3 of an acre of the planet, forgetting that God's call on our lives is to be in relationship with Him first, and then to draw others to Him second. Both the accounts of Lucifer's, and Adam and Eve's falls prove that nothing good comes from independence from God.

Our earthly relationships are meant to reflect our relationship with Jesus. Jesus went to the cross for us, placing our need for salvation above His own need to live. We depend on this for eternal life.

God does not seek to be a harsh dictator who over unfairly punishes, over taxes, and over controls. Because He created everything, He knows what is best for us and how to have an abundant life, even in a broken world. He created us to be in a loving relationship with Him, but of our own free will. He wants authenticity, intimacy and the word that most of us despise, "dependence." Yet, with total dependence on the Creator we actually find ourselves experiencing the ultimate freedom. We do as we are instructed by Him, and He promises to have all the big stuff (like eternity) covered. We are free of worry, burden, or the task of working our way into Heaven. We can be broken, and loved, and discover a new happiness within dependence.

Address the Mess:

What aspect of your life would you most desire independence from God? Be totally honest with yourself. Even if down deep, you know God's plan is best, in what way would you prefer to handle one area of your life independently?

Now, take five minutes and genuinely consider what that would look like and how you would conduct that area of your life. Would your choices be contained in their effects? What other areas of your life would be impacted by your choice to be independent in this one area, if you could be? Would the (most likely) end results be of benefit, or detriment to your life? How about the lives of those around you?

Sermon Notes

_____

_____

_____

_____

_____

_____

_____

_____

_____

_____

_____

_____

_____

_____

_____

_____

_____

_____

_____

_____

_____

_____

_____

_____

_____

_____

A Soft Place to Land

RELATIONSHIPS ARE HARD NO MATTER THE TYPE; husbands and wives, parents and kids, friends and relatives. The very best relationships are built on honesty and openness. When one party withholds facts or feelings, a breakdown begins.

At one point in my marriage facts and feelings were withheld to the point of near destruction. When truth was revealed the marriage was scarred with what seemed like irreparable wounds. Feelings of betrayal and hurt colored everything. Trust was broken and a full examination of the marriage and relationship had to take place before rebuilding could begin.

During the time of rebuilding both of us spent time with pastors, counselors, and other couples to get help and encouragement. I began a fervent study of the Bible. At the time, I chose Bible study for the fellowship with other women and because a Bible study was a heck of a lot cheaper than counseling at $150 per hour! What I didn't realize is that everything I learned in Bible study was much more valuable than anything I gained from counseling or self-help books.

In a time of prayer during this period, I was struck deeply with a question. I believe the Holy Spirit, Himself, posed this question to my heart. I heard clearly, "Are you somebody he could even confess to?" Dumbfounded and suddenly red in my face I repeated that statement to myself. "Am I someone he could even confess to?" With complete conviction, embarrassment and humiliation, my answer to God and myself was a big, fat "NO."

There are no excuses for hurting someone in a relationship, but we've all heard the saying, "hurt people, hurt people." Spouses, children, and friends need their counterparts to be someone they can come to

> *I heard clearly, "Are you somebody he could even confess to?"*

in honest confession, with all the stuff, no matter how ugly and hurtful. I realized I was not a wife my husband could come to with any sort of confession. While appearing kind on the surface, I gave off an air of superiority and I harbored a critical spirit.

At this time in our conflict we were on the road to healing but it was time for my confession. I had to fess up to not being a soft place for him to land. My attitude and hard heart only prolonged his suffering and did not bring about healing. What I learned is that my husband was full of more grace and kindness than I gave him credit for when I apologized to him. This was a turning point for us.

Address the Mess:

If you are struggling in a relationship or you suspect someone is withholding a confession that could bring about healing, ask yourself, "Am I someone they could confess to?" If you are a parent, do you scream and yell at your kids for the small stuff, making them afraid to tell you about the big stuff? If you are married, does your spouse fear your temper, snide remarks or name-calling? Do you friends always hear you criticizing others for their shortfalls, making it difficult to share their own?

James 5:16 promises us that if we confess our sins to one another, we will be healed. Healing, however, can only take place when we hear with the ears of our kind, forgiving Savior and not the ears of the judgmental Pharisee.

Sermon Notes

Calm and Calamity

THE FESTIVAL OF LESSONS AND CAROLS TOOK PLACE one year at a local college near our home and I had the opportunity to bring my three girls to enjoy it. Beginning in 1918, this worship service started at King's College in England. It is intended to be a journey through the Bible that points to Jesus's coming, highlighting various prayers and Scripture. In between each prayer and reading, a choir and orchestra take part in the telling of the Christmas story through song and music.

The festival we attended was beautiful. It was quiet and candlelit; a stark change of pace from the normal rush of the holiday season. The lady singers were dressed in Christmas finery and the men in handsome tuxedos. I was entranced by the stringed instruments that seemed to sing the sorrow and the joy we all felt. I was thankful to sit and be quiet for just a moment. It was calm amidst calamity.

Aside from the pressures of the holiday season, I admit I am weary for the state of our world. I am tired of seeing my country's flag at half-mast over and over again because of terror. I am weary from the arguing and infighting among countrymen and even among the church. But as the Scriptures rang forth, I was reminded that despite all of it, the Word came. Jesus came and He is light. The darkness will not overcome the light, even if all we see is the evidence of darkness. The readings from Genesis, Isaiah, Luke and John were all familiar to me, but last night I heard the words more clearly than ever:

In the beginning was the Word, and the Word was with God, and the Word was God. He was in the beginning with God. All things were made through him, and without him was not anything made that was made. In him was life, and the life was the light of men. The light shines in the darkness, and the darkness has not overcome it.

John 1:1-5

I needed to hear this reminder ... John 1: 9-11 says:

The true light, which gives light to everyone, was coming into the world. He was in the world, and the world was made through him, yet the world did not know him. He came to his own, and his own people did not receive him.

The light offered to everyone was not received by everyone. The peace and life offered to all men and promised for thousands of years was rejected and continues to be rejected by the very people He came to set free. I felt sad as I heard this final passage read in the Christmas story. How could there be rejection of such freely given love? Yet, this is nothing new and God knew from the beginning of time that His son would not be received by all.

The calamity is not just the shopping and baking and decorating. The calamity is the death, destruction, and rejection that at times dampens all of our hopes to half-mast. The calm is the baby that came two thousand years ago, Jesus—the Word of God made flesh, who walked among us. He loved and accepted sinners and embraced hypocrites and died for every last one of us; promising that all could have a place with Him. He overcame to become our Hope.

It's important to maintain calm amidst the calamity of this season. While I focus on Christ, there will still be presents to wrap and there will still be a tornado of unwrapping on Christmas morning. There will be groceries to purchase and prepare. There will be car rides and visits with family. There will be cranky kids in the back seat. But I recognize the weight of God's gift more clearly now than ever. We all crave the calm and peace that Jesus offers, and are invited to sit and partake, not just for an evening, or a season, but for an eternity.

Address the Mess:

Where do you feel most calm and at peace? Is there a particular geographical location, season, or event? If it is possible, make a plan to get to that place in the near future. And then, once you get there, try to learn what you can bring back home with you, so that you aren't as dependent on that particular spot to "find" peace. Jesus gives us peace. And while we may be able to better perceive Him in different places, or in different conditions, we need to look for ways to recognize His calm right in the middle of our everyday calamity.

Sermon Notes

_____

_____

_____

_____

_____

_____

_____

_____

_____

_____

_____

_____

_____

_____

_____

_____

_____

_____

_____

_____

_____

_____

_____

_____

_____

_____

Section 8

Blessed are those who are persecuted for righteousness' sake for theirs is the kingdom of heaven.

Blessed are you when others revile you and persecute you and utter all kinds of evil against you falsely on my account.

Rejoice and be glad, for your reward is great in heaven, for so they persecuted the prophets who were before you.

Matthew 5:9

Yestersay

I WAS TEXTING WITH A FRIEND THE OTHER DAY and my thumbs were flying around the keyboard of my phone haphazardly. Thankfully, the little red line appeared underneath one of the words I had typed, indicating that it was spelled wrong. Before I allowed my phone to correct the word, I stopped my typing and stared at it. The word was "yestersay." I chuckled initially, but then felt a twinge of sadness, as I was startled to realize that I have lived much of my life based on words and thoughts of the past. I would even say that there have been times that I have been tormented by "yestersay."

I have a feeling many men and women also struggle with replaying the recordings of the past. Perhaps they are replaying things that parents or siblings said, a teacher's comments, kids at school, a spouse or other relationship. Our minds are amazing tools, but the enemy's plan, (just as he tries to do with all of God's creation), is to use them against us. Instead of bringing clarification and focusing on truth, he would prefer we use our minds to indict us for "crimes" for which Christ has already done time, or to torment us with the negative impact of someone else's choices.

Here are a few of those past recordings that ruled over my personal life for far too long:

You're fat.

You're just not good enough.

No one sees you, you're invisible.

There's no way you'll be successful, why try?

You're not smart enough to do this.

Maybe some of you have heard similar recordings.

For those of us who remember and used record players long before digital recording was commonplace, we might remember how occasionally those records would get stuck in a particular spot if there was dirt, a scratch or another blemish on the vinyl. Wherever there was an imperfection, it was possible that the record needle would get stuck, and when it did, it would produce the awful result of the record playing the same part over and over again because it didn't have enough power on its own to move past the problem spot. It took someone physically picking up and moving the needle over the problematic part so that it would stop skipping. I still have memories of my dad walking over and lifting the needle off, dusting off the vinyl record and starting the song over, so it could be played to the end without skipping.

This is the perfect picture of our "yestersay" without the power of the Holy Spirit. When we accept Jesus Christ as our Lord and Savior, the Holy Spirit walks into our lives and seeks to knock that imperfection off our record so the skipping stops. Isaiah 43:18-19 says:

> *Remember not the former things,*
> *nor consider the things of old.*
> *Behold, I am doing a new thing;*
> *now it springs forth, do you not perceive it?*
> *I will make a way in the wilderness*
> *and rivers in the desert.*

While these words were spoken over the Israelites to remind them of their deliverance from Egypt by the Lord's hand, they are true for believers in Jesus Christ. With the Lord in your heart, you too, have been delivered. Not only do you have eternal life, but you have a Father in heaven who seeks to repair you and get you past the parts you are still skipping on. He wants you to know you are His child and the apple of His eye. His word trumps anything someone spoke over you that hinders you from living in freedom and doing so fully, until the end.

He says He will make a river in the desert. Rivers represent life and sustenance. Rivers are a way of traveling from one place to another. They are moving waters, and they do not get stuck. God is telling us "yestersay" words are nothing but wilderness and desert. They are dead, stuck in their conditions, and they do not give life. Remember them no more, think and meditate on Him and His word, and let Him help move you past the skipping of "yestersay," so that you can have life.

Address the Mess:

Make a list of the "yestersay" recordings you often hear on repeat. Now, share that list with a helper—a trusted friend, counselor, or pastor. Start rewriting the list with your helper. Begin to seek God's wisdom in the Bible for these areas of your life and read what God says about these areas. Ask Him to heal you, and free you, from "yestersay."

Sermon Notes

Sermon on the Mount of Messy

AFTER SOME CONTEMPLATIVE TIME OF PRAYER TODAY, I realized that I needed to make a few confessions. I was convicted in my heart about some behavior I exhibited a couple of days ago. I would like to apologize to most of the people in my neighboring small town who I likely impacted.

I decided to go to the grocery store late on Sunday morning, which was probably a big mistake. There were very few parking spots, only four carts left, and massive pallets in almost every aisle for restocking. It was like Super Bowl Sunday or the Wednesday before Thanksgiving. A slight hormonal imbalance made all of this overwhelming and downright infuriating to me. It was the perfect storm.

I have some specific confessions to make:

1) To the lady who waited patiently behind me while I agonized over which can of salty snacks to choose, I am sorry. You stood behind me so patiently and I turned and leered at you so you would go around me and get off my case! Oh my gosh, I'm sorry. It was hideous behavior. I know that because you swerved past me and sighed heavily. Truly, I don't know what overcame me, you did nothing to deserve that and maybe you had somewhere to be and my indecision about snack foods was annoying. I'm also sorry for the names I called you in my head as you rushed by.

2) To the stock guys in frozen foods, I'm sorry for cussing you out in my

head. You were just doing your job, and wouldn't I have been upset if the ice cream sandwiches weren't replenished? You can't help that the trucks came, and your manager was breathing down your neck to empty those pallets. Your manager knows good and well that angry, hormonal women are headed to that very aisle for a box of frozen antidepressants. Again, please forgive me.

3) To the lady who had to watch me cry near the cold cuts because the deli line was too long, and my daughters are growing up too fast, I'm sorry for the emotional outburst. It wasn't you, it's me. I couldn't contain my frustration about finding foods for lunch that my kids would actually eat and not let rot in the fridge for the umpteenth time. And I couldn't stop thinking that one day they'll be grown and gone, and I'll have no one who needs cold cuts.

4) Finally, I'd like to confess covetousness to the gal that walked by me. I was mad when I saw your long legs, tight bum, and cute little blazer. I wanted your freshly blown out hair instead of my air-dried frizz hair. I felt like I looked like I had just stumbled in from a frat party and here you were looking fabulous in the grocery store and you probably have kids at home who eat everything before the expiration date, and express huge amounts of gratitude for your continuously fine choices. They probably also load the dishwasher without asking. But you didn't exactly say or even imply anything like that, as you went by. It was all in my head. I am sorry.

And that, my friends, is why Jesus preached the Sermon on the Mount. Ok, I might be reaching here, but stay with me. In Biblical times, up until this sermon, the people of the day were living by the Ten Commandments. Don't kill, don't covet, don't cheat, don't lie, (to name a few); and most importantly to worship and love God more than anything else. And really for the most part, they probably thought they had the boxes checked and everything was cool. I bet we would have done the same. I mean what percentage of us are literally murderers? And last I checked most of us haven't sacrificed an animal to some statue in our backyards. But Jesus made this sermon to point out that just checking the boxes and covering the basics was not going to be enough to experience abundance and freedom of life in Him. He was trying to show us that those boxes are a little deeper than we think anyway. The Book of James says that we have the power of life and death on our tongue. Just imagine if I had let some of my mind out of my mouth in the middle of the grocery store.

Further, Jesus goes on to explain that anger and hatred in our hearts is just the same as murder. And looking on someone with lust who is not our spouse is just the same as adultery. Oh, the list goes on and on! Basically, He conveys that our private thoughts and the intentions behind our actions matter. Even doing good just to be a do-gooder, is a sin.

See how messy we are? Jesus didn't preach this sermon to condemn us, though. He didn't come to condemn the world, but to love and save the world. (John 3:17). Jesus was showing the crowd (us) that we can't possibly be perfect and clean enough to get along in this world or enter His father's house. In my case, I can't even get through the grocery store. And that's the very reason He came. Not to preach at us from a high hill, but to become like us and stand in the mess and then die for all of it so we can be clean and cured of the stink.

And remember, this same sermon contains the beatitudes; blessed are the poor in spirit, blessed are the hungry, blessed are peacemakers, blessed are you when others hate you. Whether you're impatient or being leered at by the nut job in the grocery store, you're blessed!

What happens in those mad moments is that we forget to rest and rely on Jesus. Perhaps we don't really know what that looks like. Most of the time for me, it's a deep breath and prayer asking for His grace. It allows me to smile and step aside, to admire and not want, to persevere and provide, without gritting my teeth. Clearly, I forgot this process on my grocery store trip. But when I think of what my Lord has given me, I can give of myself. Thankfully His mercies are new each morning and every grocery trip.

Address the Mess:

How long has it been since your last confession? No, I'm not talking about sitting inside church, telling it all to a priest. I'm talking about honest confession to yourself and God where you have fallen short. If you need to involve another person in your confession, be sure it is the one whom the offense was committed against. You're not embarking on a guilt trip—just a real honest discussion with God about how you've messed up and a sincere request for forgiveness. Approach the confession with honesty and humility to ask for His help as you face those things the next time.

Sermon Notes

_____

_____

_____

_____

_____

_____

_____

_____

_____

_____

_____

_____

_____

_____

_____

_____

_____

_____

_____

_____

_____

_____

_____

_____

_____

Mother Guilt

MY YOUNGEST ASKED ME ABOUT HER FIRST WORD ONE MORN-
ING. I looked over and honestly, I blanked. I couldn't
remember. I stammered and said, "I'll have to think of it."
Not long afterwards, she said, "Mommy, what time was I born?" Again,
I panicked. I couldn't recall. "Honey, it was in the early afternoon. Twelve
or one o'clock… I'll have to look for the pictures." Then I realized I hadn't
properly created a baby book for her because my scrap booking days were
replaced by counseling sessions. And then it was as if a dump truck slowly
backed up and raised its bed and heaped a load of guilt on me—some of
the worst guilt—mother guilt. I felt horrible that I couldn't recall these special moments my child wanted to know about her first days. The truth is,
not only do I not recall numbers very well, my littlest was born at a rough
time in my life.

At the time she was born, I was sleep deprived, and mothering her two
older sisters. My marriage was probably at its lowest point. I didn't know
exactly what was wrong, but I knew that addiction and depression were
responsible for eroding what I believed my husband and I had built during
the first ten years of marriage. My sweet, tender-hearted daughter entered
the world while I was barely surviving each day. I would send her sisters to
school and spend the better part of each day crying and wringing my hands
in despair. And now, when the questions come about her early days, it's
often her sisters who will recall things for me, because I simply don't remember.

Mother guilt. It's heaped upon us from many angles these days. Pinterest tells us our school snacks are boring, too plain, and not very nutritious. Pottery Barn catalogs mock our housekeeping and decorating skills. And let's not forget the other moms who whisper and smirk behind cellphones and sunglasses. If we're not condemning ourselves, someone is likely waiting at the chance to do it for us.

I got to thinking about moms in the Bible who might have struggled with guilt. How about Rebecca? She conspired against her own husband and oldest son and taught her favorite son how to lie to achieve a blessing. She went about favoring one child over another, which created a terrible family dynamic.

There was Moses' mother, Jochebed. She sent her little baby down the river to be raised in Pharaoh's household so he would not grow up a slave. She thought this would be his best chance at a better life. Ultimately, Moses did great things, but not without a struggle. He was once so angered and torn between his Hebrew roots and the Egyptian oppression, that he murdered a task master. I wonder if his mom felt some guilt and anguish over that ordeal.

During Easter, I considered Mary. A sweet, young mother who broke into song after receiving the news of her pregnancy from an angel. She rejoiced that her God saw her to be His servant even though she was lowly in stature. She rejoiced in the coming salvation her baby would bring. She pondered these things in her heart. But what about the cross? Like the song, "Mary Did You Know," we wonder just what ran through Mary's mind as the events of Jesus's life played out before her. Did she feel like she delivered her Son directly into the hands of a bloodthirsty enemy? I think moms could ache deeply for Mary.

Yet let's see what God did with it all. Although Rebecca set her son on a course of difficulty, Jacob later wrestled with God, was renamed Israel, and an entire nation was named after him.

Jochebed's name means "glory of Jehovah." She's the first person named in the Bible to have her name combined with God's name, "Jah." How striking that a mother who surrendered her son for the good of a people would be called "God's Glory." A bit of foreshadowing.

And finally, Mary. We know the end of her story. I dare say as gut wrenching and impossible as her situation became, she had the comfort of the resurrection. She was not only witness to the birth, death and resurrection of her Son, but the coming of the Holy Spirit. *She's the only one to have witnessed all four events.* I imagine the anguish was literally blown away by the mighty wind of her Son's spirit.

Even though I have struggled mightily with mother guilt, I know deep down it is not from the Lord. While I regret moments in our family and hurt it may have caused my kids, I cling to the fact that God works all things together for good for those who love Him and are called according to His purpose (Romans 8:28). I know that my husband and I love God, and our children do, too. Our God is much bigger than many days of dysfunction and He can weave those days into His beautiful tapestry of grace.

12:56pm. That's what time my littlest broke free into the world. That's the moment that changed my family forever. Her name is Josephine and it means, "God will add." We chose her name partly in jest because God surprised us when He added her. Little did we know that her name would mean so much more. He added constant hugs and wonder. He added a little girl who loves Him fiercely and shares her love with others so freely. God has already shown me how the struggles are being redeemed daily.

Address the Mess:

What guilt do you struggle with? If you are a believer, the Bible says there is now no condemnation to them which are in Christ (Romans 8:1). But the enemy would be really upset to learn that you fully believed that to be true.

We can often qualify or justify our own guilt because we think we should have or could have done something different. That may be the case, but that doesn't mean that God can't still work it for our good. He put these reassurances in the Bible so we would remember that we have been fully released from the guilt and condemnation that we would have remained in, if Jesus didn't go to the cross. He wants you to forget the power of that day, and instead wallow in the day you think you failed so badly.

Today, name a specific area of your life in which you struggle with guilt. Reflect on one of the many instances in the Bible where Jesus did not condemn, but rather covered the offender's sin with grace and healing. Then, take the Scripture in 1 Peter 4:8, and imagine Jesus's love literally covering your multitude of sins. You are free, today, my friend.

Sermon Notes

Behold the Turtle

"Behold the turtle. He makes progress only when he sticks his neck out."

James Bryant Conant

GROWING UP, I LIVED IN A NICE, LITTLE SUBDIVISION and the town's elementary school sat directly behind my backyard. The school's playground was like my very own and there were always kids to play with. It was a safe place to live and I was allowed to roam and play on my own at a very young age.

I liked to take my little red Radio Flyer tricycle over to the school's black top. It was painted with geometric shapes, four square courts and a round wheel that resembled railroad tracks. I loved to ride my tricycle on the black top and pretend I was part of a train or trace the shapes with my trike. There were great, huge honeysuckle bushes next to the court and I would stop and pick honeysuckle flowers to taste. I could spend hours by myself, completely entertained.

One summer day, I was riding by myself on the blacktop. A group of teenage boys walked down the hill from the school towards me. I immediately felt a bit nervous about these boys. They had long, scraggly hair and used bad words. We little kids called them "brats" and when they were around, we would run home and tell our parents "the brats" were out. But this time, instead of running home, I pretended to be invisible and just rode my tricycle. I hoped they would just pass through to the woods on the other side of the court, but they didn't.

While I was pedaling, one of the boys found a box turtle who was making its way from the woods across the black top. He called to his friends, "Hey, look! A turtle!" The boy picked the turtle up who was tucked safely in his shell and flung him across the black top the way one would skip a rock across water. The shell on his belly was smooth and flat and he skidded effortlessly across the pavement. I was horrified and plugged my ears so as not to hear the sound his shell made. The next boy picked him up and flung him back to his friend. They laughed and delighted in their newfound game. I wanted to scream and rescue the turtle but was frozen to my little tricycle. They wouldn't stop. Their throws came faster and harder and pieces of shell started breaking off. I sat there so still so they would not notice me, but I cried because I started to see the blood. After what seemed like an eternity, they stopped when there wasn't much left to throw, and they became bored. They left his little, dead body in the middle of black top and walked off into the woods laughing about what they had done.

As soon as they were out of sight, I ran over to see if I could help him. He was so bloody and broken. He was not recognizable. He no longer resembled what he was created to be. I sat by myself in the hot, summer sun and cried for him and for the evil way the boys treated him. I cried for myself because I was too afraid to stop those boys and felt so helpless. I wanted to take him home to my parents to have him fixed, but even at that young age, I knew it was too late. This is my first memory of the tragedy of death. This was the first time I encountered evil.

Many years later around the time of Easter, the Lord brought that turtle to my mind as a picture of Christ. Christ was the innocent, Lamb of God, paraded before leaders and crowds to be despised, rejected, slapped, spat upon, and beaten. Isaiah prophesied, "His appearance was so disfigured beyond that of any human being and his form marred beyond human likeness..." (Isaiah 52:14). Like my unrecognizable turtle, Christ was beaten so much that He no longer resembled the perfect man God created. And like the little turtle, He did not fight back. He endured His torture mostly in silence. His mother and his friends watched helplessly as a beloved son and friend was savagely murdered. Christ was not helpless like my little turtle,

240

He could have called upon legions of angels to rescue Him, but He did not. He endured. He gave in. He surrendered. All for our sake.

The turtle memory has always been a hurtful one for me, but today I am thankful that God married it to the memory of my gentle Savior.

Address the Mess:

If we're honest, we don't want to think about a bloodied and beaten Jesus during Lent, or any other time. We want to anticipate lilies and chocolates and glorious hymns sung in choir lofts. The hymns would be meaningless without the truth of His suffering and the flowers would not smell so sweet without the acknowledgement of His sacrifice. Take some time to remember the hard things and the unlovely side of the gospel. Contemplate the fear and the agony of the onlookers and the realization of the accusers that this truly was the Son of God. Imagine yourself in the scene. What would be your posture?

Sermon Notes

Sensitive Savior

I REALLY DON'T ENJOY CROWDS. I become very claustrophobic and easily irritated when I must participate in anything that resembles a crowd. I would rather have seats at that top of a stadium for a concert than be made to watch on the ground level with throngs of people pushing and pressing toward the stage. When I've had to travel through a crowded mall or airport with my kids, I grip their hands tightly and move quickly through, to get out as fast as I can. I'm completely focused on self-preservation in a crowd. Not so with Jesus.

Mark 5 is a chapter of much healing. In the second half of the chapter, Mark describes a scene that causes me to feel that panicky and claustrophobic!

> *A great crowd followed Jesus and thronged about him. There was also a woman who had a discharge of blood for twelve years, and had suffered much under many physicians. She had spent all that she had, and was not better, but rather worse. She had heard the reports about Jesus, and came up behind him in the crowd and touched his garment. For she said, "If I touch even his garments, I will be made well." And immediately the flow of blood dried up, and she felt in her body that she was healed of her disease. And Jesus, perceiving in himself that power had gone out from him, immediately turned about in the crowd and said, "Who*

touched my garments?" And his disciples said to him, "You
see the crowd pressing around you, and yet you say, 'Who
touched me?'" And he looked around to see who had done it.
But the woman, knowing what had happened to her, came
in fear and trembling and fell down before him and told
him the whole truth. And he said to her, "Daughter, your
faith has made you well; go in peace and be healed of your
disease."

Mark 5: 24-34

At this point in His ministry, Christ was faced with the masses on a regular basis. News of his miracles traveled fast. Word of His clear, simple, grace-filled teaching attracted the very people previously pushed aside by politics and religion. Yet this scene stands out. It is vivid. This woman with hemophilia, who likely has very little hope, and potentially no friends who care, comes and merely touches the hem of His garment, through the crowd, and He notices. I imagine her blindly clawing through legs and arms, hoping to reach and touch. Hoping this man was really who He said He was; hoping and praying this could be the moment the bleeding stops—the moment she feels full again, and the moment she feels like she belongs again.

Christ's touch brought sight to the blind and hearing to the deaf. His reaching out brought about life and resurrection. But this touch came from the woman. It came from someone who had no right to touch or reach out. Yet Jesus tells her that *her faith* made her well. It was not just His garment or body that had the power, but *her act* of reaching out, and *her act* of believing that transformed His cure to her need. Her healing was both initiated and completed because of the actions tied to *her faith*.

Only with the Holy Spirit do we have our awakening and our belief made possible. But I am struck over and over that Christ tells this woman that it was her action that set the miracle into transaction. Remember when Glenda the Good Witch tells Dorothy she had the power within her all along to leave Oz and get back to her family? I don't mean to trivialize this message from Christ, but I believe God is telling us, that He waits on us to reach out and make the first move. It's really very tender and sweet. God is not going to force Himself into our lives, He waits patiently. ✹

Finally, with all the commotion and noise of the massive crowds, Jesus is sensitive enough that He perceives the needs of this woman. His own disciples dismiss him, but He says, "No, someone touched me, someone needs me..." Thank you, God, that your Son is so sensitive that in the calamity of this world, Jesus stops and turns and looks. The moment He feels the touch and the longing, He makes Himself available. We should recognize that, in itself, as the miracle. And sometimes that miracle is accompanied by healing and blessings received in faith.

Address the Mess:

At some point in our lives we are all the woman on her knees reaching through the crowd to touch His garment. What's the one thing no one has been able to help you with? What's the question no one can answer? Right now, in the privacy of your prayer place get on your hands and knees and reach forward and speak your need. There's nothing magical or superstitious about this—it's not going to yield an instant result—but the physical posture of surrender and the vocalizing of your need will go a long way in your own walk with the Lord. See what happens within you, when you change your posture and reach out.

Sermon Notes

_____

_____

_____

_____

_____

_____

_____

_____

_____

_____

_____

_____

_____

_____

_____

_____

_____

_____

_____

_____

_____

_____

_____

About the Author

DON'T LET THE HOMESCHOOLING-MOM-GOOD-CHRISTIAN-GIRL FAÇADE FOOL YOU, Nicole is one of the messiest people you'll meet and she owns it 100%. A political science major in college, she doesn't actually like politics, or the insurance that she sold for a while afterwards. But she likes Jesus a lot. Actually, the most. So, she writes blogs about Him, and does ministry for Him, and she also runs a home-based business and makes sure He gets the glory, surprising unsuspecting people with gifts and offerings from the bounty. Always passionate about her work, Nicole also recently received the award for best GIF usage among her friends and coworkers. And she pretty much can fix anything with a loaf of her freshly-baked bread.

Nicole is a mom to three lovely daughters who are very well protected by a shockingly-handsome discerning dad who also gets the blessing of being married to Nicole. They have two fierce guard dogs appropriately named Fifi and Wilbur.

Connect with Nicole online at MountofMessy.com or on social media

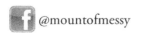 @mountofmessy    mountofmessybook

For additional copies of this book, please visit MountofMessy.com.
Also available on Amazon.com and BarnesandNoble.com.

And yes, that's Wilbur.

Made in the USA
Coppell, TX
23 February 2021